SUCCESSFUL STRATEGIC PLANNING

SUCCESSFUL

A GUIDE FOR

STRATEGIC

NONPROFIT AGENCIES

PLANNING

AND ORGANIZATIONS

PATRICK J. BURKHART
SUZANNE REUSS

SAGE Publications
International Educational and Professional Publisher
Newbury Park   London   New Delhi

For information address:

SAGE Publications, Inc.
2455 Teller Road
Newbury Park, California 91320

SAGE Publications Ltd.
6 Bonhill Street
London EC2A 4PU
United Kingdom

SAGE Publications India Pvt. Ltd.
M-32 Market
Greater Kailash I
New Delhi 110 048 India

Printed in the United States of America

Library of Congress Cataloging-in-Publication Data

Burkhart, Patrick J.
    Successful strategic planning : a guide for nonprofit agencies and organizations / Patrick J. Burkhart, Suzanne Reuss.
        p. cm.
    Includes index.
    ISBN 0-8039-4799-2
    1. Strategic planning. 2. Corporations, Nonprofit—Management.
I. Reuss, Suzanne. II. Title.
HQ30.28.B83   1993
658.4'012—dc20   92-43625
                                                                  CIP

93 94 95 96 10 9 8 7 6 5 4 3 2 1

Sage Production Editor: Judith L. Hunter

Contents

Preface

The Quest for Organizational Excellence

How would you picture the "ideal nonprofit organization"? Most of us would characterize such an organization as a purposeful, direct, successful, and financially sound enterprise that is flush with a cadre of committed personnel and volunteers. A certain brand of enthusiasm for the organization's mission would seem infectious to all who came into contact with the board and staff, and obstacles to progress would simply wither away in the face of an overwhelming consensus for action. Every client served by the organization recommends it to others in the community. Every volunteer encourages others to become personally involved with the organization. It always seems to be in the right place at the right time making good things happen.

Over the years, in both the nonprofit and profit arenas, the quest for organizational excellence and success has intensified as the level of competition for resources has increased and the corresponding odds for failure have become greater. Much like a great treasure hunt, nonprofit managers, executives, and board members devour the latest management theories in hopes of emulating the ideal nonprofit organization. Tragically for many, however, the treasure hunt never ends. Why? Generally, either nonprofit organizations do not know how to get started or the option of a "quick fix" is too attractive to ignore.

Positioning the Nonprofit Organization for Success

Long-term organizational success begins with *positioning*: that is, being postured to take advantage of a variety of critical opportunities. Positioning a nonprofit organization requires strategic planning and a commitment to realize a shared vision. Positioning is a function of all of the elements previously described for the ideal organization: clear purpose, adequate resources, enthusiasm, and commitment.

Expressions of dissatisfaction or lethargy from major stakeholders provide the major clue that a nonprofit is poorly positioned. This dissatisfaction may be manifested by a lack of board energy, fund raising difficulties, or disenchantment by clients, staff, or volunteers. Important players may have a general, if vague, feeling that somehow the organization should be more effective in addressing the variety of tasks it faces. The question then becomes, "How might the organization's effectiveness be addressed and increased?"

The Role of Strategic Planning

Strategic planning is the tool required for successful positioning and successful enterprise. It is a simple, rational method for building a consensus for participation, commitment, urgency, and action. Strategic planning is a mode of communication from within the organization to its constituencies and from the constituencies to the organization. Strategic planning cannot be accomplished from within the safety of an office or a board room. Nonprofit executives and board members must actively engage the interests of all of the organization's stakeholders. The process itself is an experience from which all nonprofits can benefit.

This workbook is intended to fill the need that thousands of small and medium-sized nonprofit agencies in the United States have for a step-by-step guide to strategic planning. These agencies generally lack the in-house expertise or the resources to hire consultants to guide and ensure completion of the strategic planning process.

In the course of working with nonprofit agencies over the years, we have observed the following universal truth: The urgency of daily problems overshadows the willingness to address fundamental organizational flaws and to pursue sound opportunities for growth. The pattern of moving from crisis to crisis and keeping the operation afloat from year to year all but precludes these organizations from taking a hard look at their missions, service delivery, staffing, competition, and sources of revenue. The irony, of course, is that if such an organization engaged in strategic planning, then some of its operational "fires" could be extinguished, and it would be free to move on to face more challenging and rewarding ventures.

We have found that the major barriers to implementation of the strategic planning process for many small organizations are beliefs that the exercise is too complex, too difficult, too lengthy, and perhaps too threatening. The available texts on the subject are indeed academic and suggest that one best be equipped with an advanced business degree to successfully complete the process.

The objective of this workbook is to demystify strategic planning: in other words, to strip the "business" veneer from the subject so that agency professionals and board members of all educational backgrounds can successfully produce a viable strategic plan and implement that plan. The necessary tools for producing a strategic plan are a clear, direct methodology and the exercise of good judgment.

Workbook Audience

Chances are that you bought this workbook because you recognize the need to produce a strategic plan for your organization. Recognizing and identifying the need for strategic planning is the first step in setting the stage to initiate what will likely be a year-long process to build a framework for the future.

You may also be using this workbook in conjunction with a fieldwork assignment that asks that you seriously and comprehensively address the capability of a nonprofit organization to plan for its own growth and continuity. The increasing numbers of failed nonprofits indicate that this issue is all too often ignored by organizations that have the best of intentions. If you plan on entering the social or human service field as a professional, then this workbook will assist you in sharpening your organizational and management skills.

Understanding strategic planning requires an acceptance of the process as an incremental set of milestones that ultimately produces a permanent commitment on the part of an organization to advance itself. This strategic planning process is more than just an expanded annual

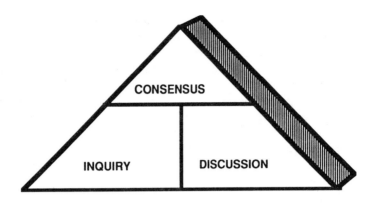

Figure P.1. The Building Blocks of Inquiry, Discussion, and Consensus

budgeting process: It is the creation and enhancement of a vision that is shared by all of your agency's key stakeholders.

Format of This Workbook

After each major section in this workbook there is a process with closure that allows the board and staff members to move forward with an ever-increasing level of knowledge about the organization and the wishes of its constituencies. The building blocks of inquiry, discussion, and consensus need to be established before a completed plan can be created (see Figure P.1).

As you proceed through the workbook, you will realize that the final step of writing the strategic plan will be one of synthesizing the materials you have developed over the course of the process. In essence, the process itself "writes" the completed strategic plan. At the end, the guesswork is removed; you will know what stakeholders think, what political agendas exist, and what opportunities lie ahead. You will be prepared to write a strategic plan that can be successfully implemented. The completed strategic plan is nothing more than the documentation of the results produced by the planning process rather than the isolated or personal creation of an enthusiastic executive director or board president.

The steps in this workbook also create a set of ancillary benefits that you should reasonably expect as outcomes of the planning process, including a renewed enthusiasm for the organization on the part of stakeholders and an intense period of visibility for the organization within the larger community.

The enthusiasm and visibility factors are enjoyable outcomes of the strategic planning process. Not only will a document be produced, but also a renewed vigor and commitment will accompany acceptance of the final product.

Overview

Organizational Symptoms That Warrant Attention

Before an organization begins the process of strategic planning, it must consider its motivation for doing so.

Frequently, the impetus to engage in strategic planning emanates from some sort of organizational problem, crisis, or sense of stagnation. When things are going well, who stops to think about more distant horizons?

Among the common symptoms that indicate the need for a nonprofit organization to begin strategic planning are the following:

- inability of a board of directors to make decisions or its tendency to delay decision making because of a lack of participation by members;
- a large board that seems to be dominated by a minority of members, which results in others feeling excluded or lacking defined roles within the organization;
- dwindling volunteer participation or donations;
- frustration resulting from internal power struggles or turf battles;
- dissatisfied clients, communities, or referral agencies;
- problems resulting from unclear roles and responsibilities for board members, staff, or volunteers;
- excessive efforts spent on resolving crises and "putting out fires."

Nonprofit Organizational Types

This workbook distinguishes small and medium-sized nonprofit organizations as belonging to one of two models: (1) the paid or professional staff model or (2) the volunteer organization model. Although these distinctions may seem simplistic, they will allow your organization to use this workbook and its examples more effectively as you work through the strategic planning process.

The Paid or Professional Staff Model

The first type of agency has a paid or professional staff that implements the policies of a volunteer board of directors. Generally, this agency provides a **service** to clients and maintains facilities where clients can either receive these services or enroll to receive them. The existence of a paid staff and facilities has prompted the organization to engage in some type of annual reporting or budgeting process, and the organization probably has a more formalized structure because of contractual funding relationships or personnel issues. With a paid staff, the volunteers will have a support function for the agency.

This workbook uses the fictional **Family House** as its example of a social service agency; it has a paid staff that provides a service to clients.

The Volunteer Organization Model

The second type of organization also has a volunteer board of directors but few, if any, paid staff. This type of organization often provides **resources** rather than services, including volunteers, expertise, funding, and materials. Generally, most of the volunteers associated with this type of organization have a commitment to the agency based on relevant personal experience. For example, health-related organizations attract volunteers who have experienced health issues personally, either themselves or through the experiences of a family member. Education-related organizations typically attract alumni or their relatives as volunteers. This second type of agency tends to be less formal in structure and may not have an established annual budgeting or planning process. Generally, the facilities are minimal, with either a small office for the organization or its business administered from a board member's home or office.

Both types of organizations may have a volunteer program in addition to a board of directors. In the absence of a paid staff, volunteers are the primary providers of the agency's resources.

This workbook uses the fictional **Community College Foundation** as its example of a volunteer-driven organization that provides resources to a school.

These models will be used throughout this workbook and will serve as useful guides to further describe the strategic planning process.

Planning and Process

The strategic planning steps outlined in this workbook are sequential (see Figure A.1). We recommend using the sequence rather than jumping around. The process provides a rational framework for accomplishing a variety of tasks, which results in a completed strategic plan. The strategic planning process relies on the creation of a strategic planning committee to accomplish the sequential tasks.

The strategic planning committee is an ad hoc committee of the board of directors, which convenes once every 3 to 5 years on a regular basis. The 3- to 5-year horizons of a strategic plan are what might be reasonably forecast about the conditions affecting the organization and its market. A longer period results in either an inaccurate plan or one so vague that it cannot be realistically implemented.

The strategic planning committee might be convened earlier than scheduled for one or more of the following four reasons:

1. an unforeseen event has altered the agency's ability to function;
2. the existing strategic plan has been completed and fulfilled more quickly than anticipated;
3. the agency's market or environment has changed dramatically, and its strategic plan's original assumptions and assessments are no longer valid; and
4. the existing strategic plan is not working and requires revision.

Once the strategic plan is produced, it becomes the responsibility of the board and staff leaders to recognize when the plan requires revision. Annual planning flows from the goals and objectives contained within the strategic plan. These goals and objectives guide the creation of

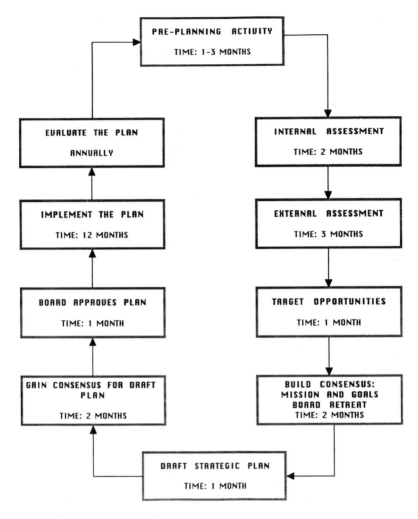

Figure A.1. Steps in the Strategic Planning Process

annual goals, objectives, and budgets that are developed by board committees and/or staff.

To be effective, the strategic plan must permeate the organization's culture and drive its work. Supervisors or committee chairs must clearly show how their annual budgets and goals relate to the strategic plan.

For this reason, everyone needs to understand the strategic plan, and it must be more than just a written document that exists separately or independently from the daily functions of the organization.

Time Frame

The planning process itself is a 12- to 15-month exercise. Can you accomplish it more quickly? Yes, but you will lose many of the inherent benefits involved in the process. This is an example where the journey is every bit as necessary and valuable as arriving at the destination.

This strategic planning process is not meant to be a full-time job for staff or volunteers. By necessity, the organization's vital work must continue through the planning process.

Strategic planning is an exercise in understanding and agreement. The length of the planning process is directly related to the number of stakeholders in the planning process. For instance, a large board with numerous constituencies will require more coordination and planning time than will a small board that serves a small population. A foundation with 45 board members and 80 identified stakeholders in the general community will require 125 contacts. The scheduling and completion of these contacts will probably take 15 months to complete. On the other hand, a small board of 15 with a stable staff and one primary referral source of clients will take much less time. In this latter example, more time may be spent analyzing client responses to inquiries rather than on volunteers or the surrounding general community.

Overview of the Family House

The Family House is a fictional nonprofit organization whose current mission is to provide temporary shelter, emotional support, and intensive clinical services to families suffering from abuse. The House provides programs and support that strive to end abusive behaviors while preserving the family.

The Family House has 10 full-time employees: an executive director, day and night managers, two clinical supervisors, and five social workers who provide direct services to client families. The House also has a volunteer program with approximately 100 volunteers who contribute time in some capacity over the course of a year.

The Family House has entered its eighth year of existence. The board of directors has term limits, and current board members have all joined within the last three years. The last of the original board members left this past year. The new board members have inherited an innovative, unique agency that has operated in relative isolation. The success of the Family House program warrants attention from others in the field.

Overview of the Community College Foundation

The Community College Foundation is more than 40 years old and a volunteer organization. The foundation was created to provide resources for the community college, and the board is primarily composed of alumni who have been appointed to positions that are more honorary than functional. The foundation has one part-time employee who handles bookkeeping.

The community college serves a large metropolitan community and has recently undergone a strategic planning process at the request of the new college president. The Foundation is not the only organization that obtains resources for the college. Over the past 10 years, athletic groups and other service organizations have obtained far more recognition for their work on behalf of the college. Thus, the mandate for the Foundation from the college is no longer clear.

The Foundation has created a modest endowment for the community college of $10 million. The new community college president has publicly challenged the Foundation to raise significant sums of money to handle the college's growing needs as its state funding remains limited. The Foundation's board members feel the need to respond to this challenge, yet they lack direction. The transition from a sleepy board to an active advocate for the community college has prompted the board to embark upon a strategic planning process.

1

Getting Started

Beginning the Process

Initiating the strategic planning process must be done with care and forethought. The desire to do strategic planning is no doubt tied to a set of perceived outcomes or benefits. Achieving these outcomes and benefits depends directly on arriving at a common understanding regarding two key issues: (1) the reasons why strategic planning is necessary and beneficial for your organization at this time and (2) how to select the best individuals to serve on the strategic planning committee.

Arriving at a common understanding of the need for organizational strategic planning requires communication skills and networking. The suggestion to engage in strategic planning may originate from one individual, a group, or a committee that has engaged in a strategic planning process in some other forum. Once the idea has been mentioned, those interested in beginning the process will need to discuss it with members of the board of directors and influential agency stakeholders. Strategic planning can then be discussed and board members exposed to it in a thoughtful and relaxed atmosphere. This may mean that those eager to begin the process will need to schedule time to meet and discuss this idea prior to a board meeting. Once a common understanding has been reached, the idea of strategic planning can be placed on a board meeting agenda and the board can begin to set the process in motion.

1

Identifying Key Stakeholders

A stakeholder is quite literally a person or group of people who have a "stake" in the organization. This stake may refer to the organization's past, present, or future. These individuals or groups may include original incorporators, previous clients, and constituencies who are currently involved in the organization or anyone who has an investment in its future. Although this may seem to be an enormous number of people, the final list will be adjusted and become more manageable as the process continues. Throughout the planning process, meetings with various stakeholders will lead to the evaluation of your organization's future. Yet the actual number of meetings, interviews, or responses will need to be of a scale that can be readily assessed by the strategic planning committee.

This chapter is concerned solely with how to determine which stakeholders would be most suitable as members of the strategic planning committee. How do you determine the "best" individuals for the task? Finding the answer to this question provides an opportunity to begin the consensus building that is a key component of the entire strategic planning process.

Within the board of directors are individuals who have influence and lend legitimacy to any effort. These members may include the current board's leadership, opinion leaders, vocal dissenters, and future leaders. You will want to take into account the existing committee structure and recruit representation from the active board committees (for example, finance, fund raising, or volunteer committees). Strategic planning is also an opportunity to groom new leaders to ensure consistent ownership of the plan over time. This will be especially important because of time limits on board terms. If everyone involved in the planning process were to leave the board within the next 12 to 18 months, who would provide the continuity so necessary to ensure that the plan is successful? A president-elect, if your organization has one, would also be an important person to have on the strategic planning committee.

As you share the strategic planning idea with board members in anticipation of a vote on the issue, you will also want to solicit and discuss ideas for the strategic planning committee. The committee should have between 5 and 10 permanent members who will remain with the process for the 12-month duration. At various stages in the process, other individuals may be called on to assist with tasks in areas of specific expertise, but the committee itself needs to be large enough to address the scope of issues affecting the organization while small enough to allow active participation by everyone.

The strategic planning process is not meant to be a single-focus exercise. Members of the committee may no doubt have specific areas of interest, but they must be willing and eager to address a wide array of issues. A good idea is to have at least one member of the committee be a relative newcomer to the organization, someone who lacks a strong historical affiliation with the agency. A newcomer, if comfortable in the committee, may be more able to ask "Why?" than someone who has created or developed the existing system.

Devising a Structure for the Process

Before the strategic planning committee can begin its work, the board must give a clear mandate to the committee about what it is empowered to do and what type of product will be produced from the effort. Depending on your board's style of handling business, this can be accomplished in two different fashions: (1) by providing the mandate at the same time that the board votes to begin the strategic planning process or (2) by approving the concept of strategic planning and allowing the executive committee to return to the board and present the completed mandate once the committee is established.

This strategic planning committee mandate involves writing a brief statement that identifies:

- why the committee is convening,
- what the committee is expected to produce,
- to whom the committee is accountable, and
- what types of support or resources will be made available to the committee.

The strategic planning committee may be accountable to the board's president or to the executive committee, and the manner in which the strategic planning committee will report its progress must be identified clearly. If the strategic planning committee will generate quarterly reports or provide quarterly briefings, then this schedule needs to be established.

The roles of staff or volunteer support services for the strategic planning committee also must be clarified. If a strong, capable staff exists, then the strategic planning committee may be instructed to primarily lend critical thinking, analysis, and appraisal to the staff work. If no staff support is available, then the committee members will need to assume such responsibilities as data gathering, analysis, and clerical support. In either case, the strategic planning committee may require a budget for the process. Although the actual budget may be difficult to produce before the strategic planning committee is formed, the format for submitting a budget needs to be clarified.

The anticipated schedule of the strategic planning process should also be included in the committee mandate. If you choose to follow the time frame identified with the process in the Overview (see Figure A.1), you can anticipate that the strategic planning committee will be active for 12 months. The creation, presentation, and acceptance of the plan in the fall will allow the board committees and staff or volunteers to incorporate the goals and objectives into their annual planning process. Chapter 10 also provides an overview of the annual planning process. With this schedule, the plan can be implemented in January with the full support of everyone involved in the organization. If your organization has a different fiscal year, you can shift the time frame accordingly, beginning the preplanning activities 1 to 3 months before the start of your fiscal year.

Sample Board Mandates for Strategic Planning Committees

Family House

Discussion: The Family House conducted its preplanning activities in two steps. First, two resolutions were presented to the board to begin a strategic planning process. Once the resolutions were approved, the executive committee met and drafted a mandate about the specifics of the planning process for the board's approval.

Family House Board of Directors Mandate for the Strategic Planning Committee

RESOLVED that the Family House Board of Directors will create an ad hoc Board committee, the Strategic Planning Committee, which will lead the House to create a strategic plan. RESOLVED that the Executive Committee will draft guidelines and expectations to provide a format and guide for the Strategic Planning Committee.

STRATEGIC PLANNING COMMITTEE GUIDELINES

The Board of Directors of Family House has approved a resolution to initiate and conduct a year-long strategic planning process. The broad goals of this process include:

- evaluation of agency effectiveness in serving community needs, and
- evaluation of organizational effectiveness internally.

The Strategic Planning Committee will function for a 12-month period, beginning January 199x and ending December 199x. The Committee will be composed of eight permanent members who will be nominated next month during our regular annual nominating process.

The Strategic Planning Committee will report to the Executive Committee on a quarterly basis in the same fashion as other regular Board committees. The Executive Committee will issue a meeting schedule for all committees at their first meeting in January 199x.

The Strategic Planning Committee will be expected to produce a working budget for the year-long process in the same manner as other standing committees. The Executive Director will staff this Committee and be a nonvoting member of the Committee. The Executive Director will ensure that the Committee receives adequate clerical support and will assist the Committee in developing a working budget to address these needs.

The Strategic Planning Committee will provide interim working summaries of its activities in conjunction with the planning process. The following schedule identifies the tasks and reporting requirements of the Committee.

Schedule

- an internal assessment, duration two months, working summary to Board at regular March meeting;
- an external assessment, duration three months, working summary to Board at regular June meeting;
- a Board retreat to be held in August; the Committee will prepare the structure of the retreat and include data and information necessary to (1) evaluate the external and internal assessments and (2) create goals and objectives for the strategic plan.

The Committee will prepare a draft strategic plan for discussion by the regular September meeting. This draft will be made available to all committees, staff, and volunteers to evaluate and include in their own annual planning.

The Committee will solicit responses and revise the plan in time for final approval of the plan at the December annual meeting.

Community College Foundation

Discussion: The Community College Foundation conducted its pre-planning activities before its board resolved to begin the strategic planning process. The foundation has a very active executive committee that conducts most of the board's business. The executive committee prepared the following paper, which was distributed one month before the planned board meeting. The entire paper was approved by the board.

COMMUNITY COLLEGE FOUNDATION BOARD OF DIRECTORS MANDATE FOR THE STRATEGIC PLANNING COMMITTEE

The Board of Directors of the Community College Foundation has been challenged by our new Community College President to aggressively raise funds for the Community College to:

- meet anticipated cutbacks in state funding and
- prepare to expand the current College programs and facilities.

The Foundation Board believes that this challenge will require significant strategic planning to implement. With this in mind, the Board will convene an ad hoc committee, the Strategic Planning Committee, to engage in a year-long process. This Committee will be composed of the five vice-chairs of the standing committees. College faculty and staff will be called upon to assist this process, and the President has assured us that he will assist in gaining their participation. The Chair of the Strategic Planning Committee will become a member of the Executive Committee and will report monthly on the Committee's progress.

The Strategic Planning Committee will conduct a Board retreat this summer. The data and evaluations that have been conducted in the planning process will be presented to the Board at this retreat.

A draft strategic plan will be issued in September for discussion by the Board. The completed and revised plan will be submitted prior to the annual meeting in December for final Board approval.

RESOLVED that the Board of Directors of the Community College Foundation will conduct and complete a strategic plan during the calendar year 199x.

2

Internal Assessment

Framing the Internal Assessment

The internal assessment is an exercise that provides the organization with a profile of what the organization thinks about itself. This strategic planning workbook begins with an internal assessment because it is vital for the strategic planning committee to first understand what the internal stakeholders believe about the organization, including its mission, effectiveness, and direction, as well as the perceived needs of the external constituents.

Three broad areas of organizational performance will be evaluated during the internal assessment. The first is the **resources** available or needed to perform the work of the organization. These resources can be human (staff or volunteers), financial (cash or in-kind), or capital (equipment and facilities). The second area is the **performance** of the organization's components in accomplishing the organization's overall work. Organizational performance tends to be minimized by internal stakeholders, while external stakeholders use it as a major criterion for evaluation. Performance reflects the organization's capacity for effectively addressing the needs it was created to meet. The third area is **process**, which focuses on the strategies and methods used to provide the organizational services or resources. Process issues most often deal with organizational structure and the communications between components of the organization.

Internal Perceptions of Organizational Performance

"Where should we go as an organization?" To answer this question, you must first understand what stakeholders believe about your organization. You must determine the perceptions of the organization's past, present, and future as identified by internal stakeholders.

As you complete the internal assessment, you will compare the perceptions of the organization with the specific facts and evaluate the accuracy of these perceptions. The inaccuracies may point the way to a clear set of priorities that need to be addressed through the planning process.

Internal stakeholders include board members, volunteers, and staff-members who maintain the organization's structure and work. Each stakeholder may tell a different story about the agency's performance, allocation of resources, and process. The outcome of the internal assessment is a profile that evaluates these "stories" and identifies areas that may offer opportunities for growth or change.

An example of potential disparity between perceived performance and actual performance clarifies this exercise. If the internal stakeholders feel that the organization is doing poorly because relatively few clients are served and yet agency data indicate that the client base has increased substantially over time, then you have an issue that requires attention. Perhaps the internal stakeholders are unaware of the range of client services offered or fail to realize that the presenting need is so great that one organization cannot hope to address it effectively. In either case, you will have a list of issues that require additional attention from an external assessment before you create a strategic plan.

Components of the Internal Assessment

The internal assessment has four basic components:

1. a board of directors assessment,
2. a staff assessment (if applicable),
3. a volunteer assessment, and
4. a statistical review that includes (a) a financial profile and (b) a service evaluation.

The purpose of the internal assessment is to combine these four components into a coherent statement about the organization. Although some disparity between the components may be seen, these disparities will provide valuable information. If the various stakeholders have vastly different perceptions about the organization, then there may be a communication or coordination issue that requires attention.

Resources: Financial and Budget Assessments

The internal assessment is an exercise that evaluates internal perceptions of your organization. The accuracy of these perceptions and the ability to determine which perceptions require action implies that the organization be assessed in terms of financial resources and their impact on the provision of services or resources.

To illustrate this issue in a concrete fashion, the absence of sufficient resources in a nonprofit may preclude an effective response to the needs of the clients or entities served by the organization. If a volunteer organization lacks the tools to effectively provide resources to the community, then the organization actually is unable to perform the tasks for which it was created. The volunteer capability may be sufficient, but the necessary support functions may lack funding or be so minimal as to negate the effectiveness of the volunteer effort.

Similarly, in a service agency, the absence of sufficient resources may limit staffing or prevent the agency from acquiring facilities that would adequately serve the clients. All nonprofits tend to believe that greater funding would solve all of their pressing needs. Too often, however, this search for funding is done in the absence of clear, strategic thinking about the overall organizational needs for resources. Without a comprehensive evaluation of the current resources or lack thereof, the organization is ill prepared to pursue funding options that may arise. The internal assessment, however, deals solely with the organization's identified needs or desires for enhanced resources. The internal assessment may identify needs that may be appropriate for further discussion and ultimately may lead to the pursuit of funding at a later date.

Process: Organizational Structure

The process by which your organization is able to effectively address its mission and associated tasks is directly related to the formalized structure that guides the agency's operations. The organizational structure can either enhance service or resource delivery or serve to frustrate clients, supporters, or contributors. For example:

- Is the board able to set policies that reflect the needs of the clients as well as the capabilities of the staff?
- When the staff are aware of new needs, is the board's process of evaluating options easily accessible?
- If the volunteers have concerns, are staff and the board responsive to these issues?
- If the agency has more than one location, do the outlying areas feel represented or isolated from the central office?

You will want to determine if your structure is responsive to new ideas, problems in the field, and the interests of various stakeholders. Essentially, organizational structure is a formal communications network. Analyzing organizational structure is a way to determine how well the different components of the agency communicate in accomplishing their tasks.

This information may best be acquired through the responses received from interviews with your internal stakeholders. The survey instruments are designed to provide a broad area of discussion. In the course of the interview, if you learn of issues that are relevant to your organizational structure, then information can be presented separately to elicit greater attention.

Analyzing the present structure may provide clues for organizational change. An organizational chart should be included in your internal assessment, regardless of whether a specific change is being considered. The organizational chart can be as simple or as detailed as desired.

Depending on your organization, you may choose either to have a detailed representation of board and volunteer committee relationships or to focus on the primary relationships between board and staff. Examples for both of our sample organizations are shown in Figures 2.1 and 2.2.

Performance: Service Delivery Assessment

A service delivery assessment provides the additional information that creates a context for your financial assessment. The service deliv-

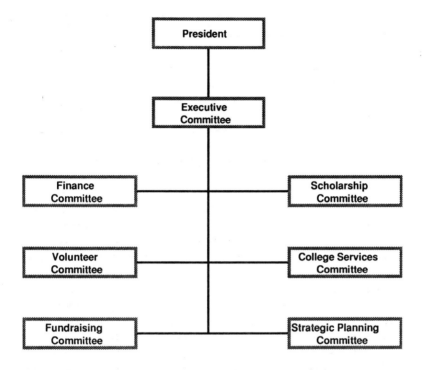

Figure 2.1. A General Organizational Chart (Community College Foundation)

ery system assessment answers the question, "Who do we serve and what do we provide in services or resources?"

Defining *who* your agency serves requires some agreement about the numbers that will be used. For example, if you provide family services as well as programs for children and adults, you will need to decide how to count your clients. If a family goes through an intake process and then receives one or more services, then you may be inclined to only count the total number of families served in a given period. However, the levels at which different families use your agency services may vary considerably. You may wish to have one summary category for *families served* and other categories such as *children served*, *adolescents served*, and *adults served*. These latter categories might best be identified by program name. A simple service delivery assessment is shown in Table 2.1.

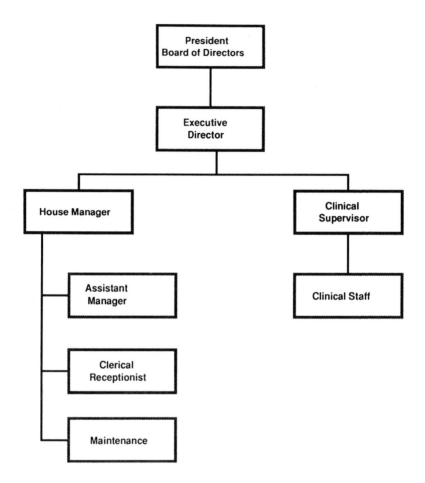

Figure 2.2. A More Detailed Organizational Chart (Family House)

The point of this numeric breakdown is not to overcount your client base, but to provide clarification about the types of programs within the agency that are being used. In addition, the organization may decide later to expand a program when enrollment figures allow a reasonable assessment of the potential expansion. Service delivery assessments for our two sample organizations are provided in Tables 2.2 and 2.3.

Table 2.1 A Simple Service Delivery Assessment

May 199x
Total families served: 35
Program enrollment
    Sibling workshop: 12
    Boys club: 8
    Girls club: 9
    Parenting class: 20
    Teen group: 5

Table 2.2 Service Delivery Assessment for Family House

May 199x
Total families residing in Family House this month: 15
Adults residing this month: 30
Children residing this month: 45
Average family size: 4
Average length of stay (weeks): 3
Referral sources
    Child protective services: 9
    Courts: 4
    Domestic violence shelter: 1
    Hospitals: 1
Location of family home
    Johns County: 12
    Peters County: 3
Family fees paid by
    Insurance: 10
    Private: 3
    State: 2

Table 2.3 Service Delivery Assessment for Community College Foundation

May 199x
Scholarships awarded this month
   Liberal arts: 2
   Work study: 5
   Internships: 2
Average scholarship amount ($): 1,000
Average length of scholarship (months): 6
Scholarship recipients
   Males: 5
   Females: 4
Ethnic background of recipients
   Native American: 3
   Asian: 1
   Black: 2
   Hispanic: 1
   White: 2
Volunteer services
   Campus speaking engagements: 5
   Community speaking engagements: 15
   Volunteer hours this month: 100

3

Internal Assessment Tools and Instruments

Creating the Survey Instruments

The basic questions raised in the internal assessment about the organization will require different "framing" for the different stakeholders, taking into account their relative involvement in a particular area. However, the basic issues that make up the components of the internal assessment will remain the same. The survey instruments will need to query the respondents on the three broad issues of resources, performance, and process.

Survey Instrument: Board of Directors

While building the survey instruments, you will need to address a wide array of issues that are involved in the internal operations of the organization. To begin, we focus on the issues that may be relevant for your board of directors.

In a nonprofit organization, the board's role is to advance the organization in the community and to provide guidance and expertise in policy, fiscal, and legal issues. By advancing the organization in the community, the board advocates issues of concern to the organization,

Table 3.1 Specific Issues Limiting Organizational Success

Time: Board members may not have enough time in their schedules to advance the needs of the organization successfully. They may be so involved in specific tasks that they fail to view the organization's broader needs and their implications.

Commitment: Board members may not understand or accept the organization's financial and program needs. Members may be appointed to the board because of their affiliations with other organizations. In some instances, such affiliations frame their involvement and limit their activities to issues that directly concern outside affiliations. Members also may have been recruited to the board without a clear orientation to the organization's greater needs.

Skills: Board members may have good intentions but be relatively inexperienced in addressing unique organizational and client needs. Thus, the board as a whole may have difficulty in planning and implementing successful programs.

Strategic plan: Without a comprehensive plan or guide, board members lack orientation and are unable to direct their participation along the most appropriate avenues.

Materials: The board may lack the necessary tools for specific activities, such as clerical support, office space, or equipment.

Size: The board may be too small or too large to effectively conduct its business. On a very small board, the level of commitment required of each member may become too draining over time. On a large board, the members may lack a sense of personal commitment and feel themselves to be "outsiders" to the program. Members may perceive that organizational politics create "in" and "out" groups.

---

raises public awareness of the problem related to the organizational mission, and raises funds for program efforts. How well each board performs is related to the willingness of individual members to volunteer time and expertise. In some cases, the board may intend to assist the organization but lack the skills to do so successfully.

An organization may have difficulty with programs or fund raising for several reasons. If you are uncertain about the specific issues confronting your board, the issues identified in Table 3.1 may help you define the problem.

Board members are key stakeholders in the organization, so determining why an individual is on the board and what he or she hopes to receive from involvement are important issues. If you overlook these issues, then you may find yourself struggling to accomplish tasks, never realizing that the task may in some way jeopardize the board member's continued involvement. Each board member needs to be asked the following questions:

Why are you serving on the board?

What other affiliations will affect your actions on the board?

Table 3.2 A Sample Board Survey

1. How many years have you served on the board? How did you become involved with the board of directors? Has the board or our organization changed over the course of your involvement? How do you feel about these changes?
2. Have you held any chairs or officerships during your involvement?
3. How would you classify your participation as a board member: very active? active? occasionally active? seldom active?
4. Please describe our organization's mission.
5. How effective have we been in fulfilling this mission?
6. What are the major strengths of our organization?
7. What are the major weaknesses of our organization?
8. What do you believe are the strongest opportunities facing our organization over the next 3 to 5 years? Why?
9. What roles should individual board members play in advancing our organization?
10. What role would you like to play?
11. What do you need to better assist you in performing your tasks for the board?
12. What would you like to see our organization accomplish within the next 3 years? the next 5 years?
13. What key issues need to be addressed in this strategic planning process?

Have you had personal experiences with the services offered by the organization? If so, what were they?

What personal goals do you have for the organization?

A sample board survey is presented in Table 3.2. It combines the various elements discussed throughout this chapter. The survey has three subsections, the purpose of each being to provide information relevant to the planning process. The first three questions address demographics related to the individual being interviewed. This information may be helpful later in painting broad pictures of types of individuals who provide certain responses. Questions 5 through 9 address the organizational purpose and effectiveness. The final questions ask the individual to conceptualize how the organization will arrive at change(s) and focus on future directions that the organization may take.

Table 3.3 A Sample Staff Survey

---

1. How long have you worked for our agency? Has our agency changed during the time you have been here? How do you feel about these changes?

2. Have you worked in different jobs over that time?

3. How did you become involved in the agency? Did you have a relationship with the agency before your employment?

4. What aspects of our agency help you do your job?

5. What aspects of our agency hinder you from doing your job?

6. Please describe our agency's mission.

7. How effective have we been in fulfilling this mission?

8. What are the major strengths of our agency?

9. What are the major weaknesses of our agency?

10. What would you like to see our agency accomplish within the next 3 years? within the next 5 years?

11. What do you believe are the greatest opportunities facing our agency at this time?

12. What key issues need to be addressed in this strategic planning process?

Survey Instrument: Staff

In organizations that provide services through a professional staff system, the staff members are also key stakeholders in the organization. Each organization is somewhat unique in the way it defines board and staff responsibilities. The staff generally provides services and carries out the board's policies. The staff also interacts directly with the client population and has a more immediate awareness of the need for services.

Staff responsibilities may include operational duties (such as supervision and management), internal agency duties (operating the facilities and service delivery), and community duties (managing or recruiting volunteers and handling public relations).

In addition to the questions asked of board members, the assessment must address several broad indicators for staff performance:

- general satisfaction with the work environment and associated tasks;
- levels of absenteeism or job turnover rates; and
- proficiency within assigned tasks, or the ability to complete assignments in a timely and comprehensive manner.

Table 3.4 Family House Volunteer Survey

1. How long have you been a volunteer for the House?
2. How did you become involved in our volunteer program?
3. How would you classify your participation as a volunteer: very active? active? occasionally active? seldom active?
4. Has the House changed in any way since you have been involved? How do you feel about these changes?
5. Please describe the House's mission.
6. How effective have we been in fulfilling this mission?
7. What are the major strengths of our organization?
8. What are the major weaknesses of our organization?
9. What do you believe are the biggest opportunities facing the volunteer program over the next 3 to 5 years? Why?
10. What would you like to see our volunteers accomplish within the next 3 years? the next 5 years?
11. What aspects of our House provide you with the most satisfaction as a volunteer?
12. What frustrations have you had as a volunteer at our House?
13. What do you need to better assist you in performing your volunteer tasks?
14. What key issues need to be addressed in this strategic planning process?

The staff survey also focuses on three subsections—demographics, mission effectiveness, and future directions—in a manner that is consistent with the board survey (see Table 3.3).

Survey Instrument: Volunteers

Many nonprofit organizations have one or more groups of volunteers who actively support the organization. At a minimum, these volunteers may be regular financial donors; at a maximum, they may perform duties as comprehensive as any staff or board member.

Depending on the structure of your organization, the volunteer survey may replace a staff survey, resemble a board survey, or be a combination of the two. To remain consistent with the previous interviews, the volunteer survey also asks questions that are related to demographics, mission effectiveness, and future direction. Our two sample organizations have quite different volunteer programs, and their survey instruments (see

Table 3.5 Community College Foundation Volunteer Survey

1. How long have you been a volunteer for the Foundation? Has the Foundation changed during your involvement? How do you feel about these changes?

2. How did you become involved in our volunteer program?

3. How would you classify your participation as a volunteer: very active? active? occasionally active? seldom active?

4. What do you need to better assist you in performing your tasks for the Foundation?

5. Please describe the Foundation's mission.

6. How effective have we been in fulfilling this mission?

7. What are the Foundation's major strengths?

8. What are the Foundation's major weaknesses?

9. What do you believe are the biggest opportunities facing the Foundation over the next 3 to 5 years? Why?

10 What roles should individual volunteers play in advancing the Foundation?

11. What role would you like to play?

12. What would you like to see the Foundation accomplish within the next 3 years? the next 5 years?

13. What key issues need to be addressed in this strategic planning process?

Tables 3.4 and 3.5) help to illustrate this issue. The Family House uses volunteers to assist staffmembers, while the Community College Foundation uses volunteers instead of paid staff.

Interviews and Questionnaires

The survey instruments can be used either as personal interviews or as written questionnaires. The decision about appropriate format depends on several issues as well as potential audiences.

Ideally, the board surveys should be done as personal interviews. Personal contact will be valuable in building consensus for the planning process. Generally, a written questionnaire should be reserved for those board members who are inaccessible for interviews, although a board member who is continually inaccessible may no longer be suitable for board membership. This issue in itself may be a valuable discussion topic for the planning committee.

Staff may have personal issues that would limit their candor in an interview setting. If your committee believes this may be the case, then you may decide to use a confidential questionnaire.

Depending on the organization, volunteers once again may resemble the board or the staff in survey format. A large volunteer program may require that you combine formats and use a personal interview for a group of volunteers and a written questionnaire for less active volunteers. One note of caution: If many of the volunteers are inactive, then they may be unwilling to respond to a written questionnaire. Once again, this may be a good issue for the planning committee to address because inactive volunteers may lack sufficient commitment to advance the organization.

Conducting Personal Interviews

Personal interviews are valuable because they increase the involvement of the individuals in the planning process. The strategic planning committee will need to prepare for the personal interviews with greater detail and attention than they would for a written questionnaire.

Before scheduling the interviews, the committee needs to discuss who will conduct the interviews and establish a structure for the interviews. The committee may decide that certain members are best suited to conduct them or that the list of individuals will be divided in some fashion among the committee members. Clearly, this is no time to send committee members to interview individuals with whom they have long-standing disagreements.

The interviews themselves need to be scheduled conveniently and conducted without interruptions. The location of the interview needs to increase the ease of discussion as well as allow the respondent to comfortably schedule the interview during his or her day.

The committee should determine whether the interviews will be recorded or if notes will be made during the process. In either case, the interview style should be as nonintrusive as possible to allow a natural and easy conversation. In addition, the committee needs to determine how the interview will be used, and this information should be shared with the respondent when the interview is being scheduled. If the interviews are confidential and will never be shared outside the committee in raw format, then this may elicit greater candor in the responses. If the interviews are to be shared with the board, then this fact and the format for releasing the interview information must be explained. If responses are to remain confidential, then use a coding system that will protect the identities of those being interviewed. The coding system can be as simple as designating letters or numbers rather than the respondent's name in any interview materials.

Tips for Conducting Personal Interviews

The interviewer must be a good listener and maintain a clear interest in understanding the information and perceptions conveyed by the respondent. Before the interview, the interviewer will need to make sure that all materials needed for the interview are present and that he or she is well prepared.

The interviewer also must understand what the respondent believes about the agency and why a particular belief is held. For example, if a board member states that the agency is ineffective in pursuing its mission, then the interviewer will want to know the following:

- relevant anecdotal information,
- personal experiences,
- isolated instances, and
- information about general breakdowns in communication or service delivery.

The interviewer's role is to elicit responses to the questions in an open-minded, nonjudgmental fashion. If unusual information is related, then this is not the appropriate time to dispute it or attempt to change someone's mind. One would more appropriately seek clarification and best attempt to understand what is being conveyed. The interviewer does not need to agree with a particular perspective, but acknowledging that an individual may be feeling frustrated or unhappy about an issue of importance to them may be helpful. An interviewer also may hear of great successes that have been ignored or not evaluated in the same way by the organization. Such instances also may provide valuable information for the strategic planning committee to evaluate.

Tips on Handling Questionnaires

If you decide to use written questionnaires, the committee will need to choose the type of cover letter that will best encourage a response. The cover letter should convey the importance of the questionnaire to the overall strategic plan and should be signed by the chair of the strategic planning committee. In general, getting everyone to mail a questionnaire back to the organization is very difficult. One way around this problem is to distribute the questionnaires at a time when they can be answered and returned at one sitting. In addition, stamped and addressed envelopes should be included with the questionnaire. Once again, if the responses are to remain confidential, the questionnaire should not solicit the respondent's name. An open space for comments at the end of the questionnaire also may be desirable; this would allow the respondent to provide any additional information that he or she may deem relevant.

Financial Assessments

The information that you need to produce will essentially answer the question, "How are we doing financially and what preparations are required to plan for our organizational future?" These assessments require that you gather statistics about your organization and present them in a fashion that is understandable to your audience.

Many individuals involved in nonprofit organizations feel uncomfortable about using and evaluating statistics. This section will assist you in preparing your statistics in a relatively easy manner. The key point is that the result of your efforts needs to be comprehensible to your stakeholders. Essentially, you must evaluate areas that are relevant to the organizational stakeholders and present them in a fashion that allows thoughtful discussion and response.

To evaluate your current financial picture, you will want to address your annual budget in terms of revenue and costs. If you do not already provide some type of monthly or quarterly budget report, then you may have to create this information by returning to your ledger or checkbook and breaking out the information in monthly or quarterly periods. A simple organizational financial assessment for summarizing your actual income and expenses would look like that shown in Table 3.6. The Actual column shows what actually occurred, the Budget column is what you had anticipated, and the Variance column shows the difference between the Actual and Budget columns. If you received less income than you had budgeted, then the variance number will be a negative number (a loss in projected income). If you spent more than you had budgeted, then the variance also will be a negative number.

Table 3.6   A Simple Organizational Financial Assessment

	Actual	Budget	Variance
Income			
Client Fees			
Grants			
Donations			
Fund Raising or Special Events			
Other			
Total Income			
Expenses			
Salaries			
Employee Related Benefits			
Rent/Mortgage			
Utilities			
Telephone			
Janitorial			
Office Supplies			
Program Supplies			
Board and/or Volunteer Program Costs			
Insurance			
Legal/Accounting			
Maintenance			
Travel			
Other			
Total Expenses			
Net Total (Income Less Expenses)			

The variance column will provide you with interesting and valuable information. If your income is much lower than anticipated, then the strategic planning committee will need to identify what occurred that was not anticipated. In the same fashion, if your expenses are higher than budgeted, then the committee will need to know why the budget was inaccurate and what changes, if any, will be needed in future budget planning. If you have received more income and spent less than your budget, then this also needs to be evaluated.

Many organizations experience seasonal changes in income and expenses, so at the very least you will want to construct quarterly evaluations for the current year to note any seasonal changes. For example, client fees might drop during summer because referral sources are less active or on vacation. The strategic planning committee may then wish to plan activities to compensate for these seasonal changes if they are a source of concern.

Once you have completed this evaluation for the current year, you would do well to look at the previous year as well. The chart would look the same, but the column headings would read Current Year, Last Year, and Variance.

The Variance column also can be presented as a percentage change. You could do this for any large variance in a category, or you could just use the total expense, total income, and total variance numbers. The percentage of the variance is calculated by this formula:

$$Percentage = Variance \div Budget$$

for the current year, or

$$Percentage = Variance \div Last\ Year$$

for the two-year analysis. If the variance is a negative number, then percentage change is also a negative number and represents the percentage loss. If all of the numbers are positive, then the percentage change is a gain.

Format for Financial Assessment

The information from your assessments can be presented either in numerical chart format or graphed, which also may be a useful way to

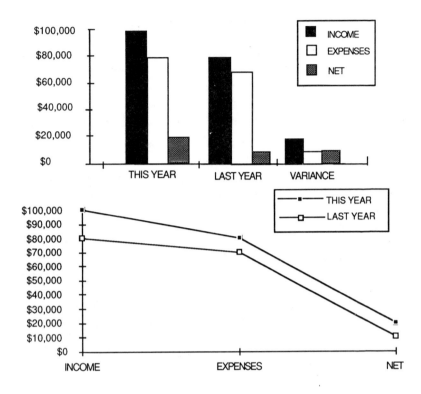

Figure 3.1. Sample Graphs of Financial Assessment Information

convey the same information. Figure 3.1 shows two examples of easily created and easily read graphs.

If you decide to graph your data, try to choose numbers that are meaningful and show the reader the point you are trying to convey. A chart with all of your budget details would be impossible to read and thus not at all helpful. The chart should summarize and indicate changes in a broad sense.

Whether you use charts or graphs, the assessment should also contain a written narrative that explains any areas of particular interest. Significant changes in specific categories, such as the seasonal change discussed earlier, need to be addressed in an accompanying narrative.

Client and Recipient Information

The service delivery assessment should also "paint a picture" of your clients or recipients. This information will vary depending on the type of service or resource being provided.

Presenting the Service Delivery Assessment

The monthly data that you have collected should be formatted to closely resemble the financial assessment previously prepared. If possible, create summary tables that represent the current year, the past year, and the variance between the two (as described previously). The summary tables will then be possible to graph in a similar manner as the budget assessment.

Once again, keep in mind that the information needs to be easily understood by your audience, so your graphs or tables should convey useful information and indicate any broad changes. Do not graph all of the data elements included in the summary tables. Once again, these changes should be addressed in an accompanying narrative; they may describe issues that require further inquiry by the strategic planning committee. Our two sample organizations and their graphed delivery assessments are shown in Figure 3.2. Sample internal assessments for both Family House and Community College Foundation are presented below.

Family House: An Internal Assessment

The Family House provides services to families in abusive situations. Sadly, we have no "typical" client. For spousal abuse, parents usually have only a high school education, although 25% have some higher education. Generally, the mother is a homemaker, and the family income level ranges from lower to upper middle class, dependent on the father's earning level. Marriages are generally 10 to 15 years in duration, and there are 2 to 3 children per family. For child abuse, we see no clear trends, but most victims (75%) are girls, and the abuse has occurred primarily from a family member or boyfriend living in the home. For elderly abuse, most families are middle class but lack the financial resources to place elderly relatives in a supervised living arrangement. Most of our clients (80%) have been referred to treatment at least twice before they entered the Family House program.

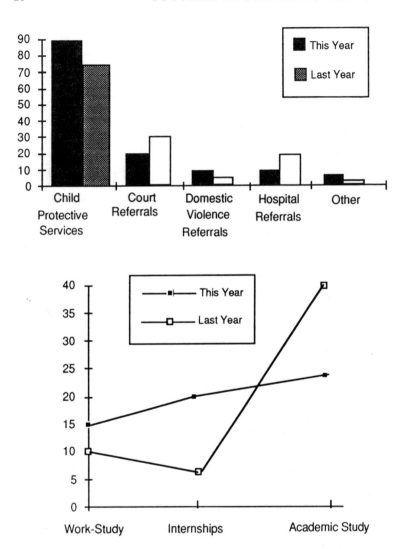

Figure 3.2. Graphs of Family House's Service Delivery and Community College Foundation's Resource Delivery Assessments.

The vast majority of the adults involved come from abusive homes and are repeating a pattern of abuse. Families come to the

House seeking control and relief from their abusive and frequently escalating problems. Families who enter our program are generally quite compliant with treatment, especially because their only other option may be court-ordered separation. Families generally remain in the House for 6 to 8 weeks of intensive care followed by aftercare in their home with subsequent monitoring continuing for 8 months as an aftercare program.

The unique feature of our program is that families remain intact throughout the treatment and aftercare follow-up. The recidivism rate is exceedingly low: 90% of the families that complete the entire program remain abuse-free 18 months after completing the program. Approximately 10% of all families accepted into the House fail to complete the entire program. Once a family fails to comply with the program, it is not eligible to return. The waiting list and need for services are too great to allow repeated attempts at intervention for families that lack the motivation to comply with program objectives.

While families are living in the House, they are encouraged to maintain all aspects of their independent living obligations; children attend school and parents continue with their jobs or training programs. Families cook their own meals at the House and are responsible for housekeeping details in their living quarters. Families are allowed to bring small household pets with them, provided that they maintain their living environments and do not produce an unreasonable burden on other families residing in the House.

BOARD OF DIRECTORS

The Board of Directors of the Family House played a strong leadership role in the creation and design of the original program. Currently, the Board's responsibilities include the following:

- policy making (bylaws, rules, and personnel policies),
- organizational oversight (budgeting, planning, auditing, and recruiting new Board members), and
- operational involvement (fund raising, public relations, and special events).

Policy and organizational tasks have been handled exceedingly well because of the roles of key Board members with extensive experience in handling these matters. However, the Board as a whole expressed a concern about a lack of direction and frequently becomes consumed with the details of agency management rather than seeing the agency holistically. Operational issues have been less consistent and clearly dependent on the committee chair's capabilities and commitment. In the past two years, fund raising and special events have been quite successful, primarily because of the leadership skills of the committee chairs. However, no plans are in place to train new chairs or Board officers to replace these positions when current terms of office expire.

The Board needs a workstation at the House with a computer and phone to increase commitment and purpose. The Board members need a program for developing leadership skills to ease the transition of committee chairs and officers. The Board needs an orientation packet for new members that clearly explains the time and expertise required to successfully fulfill Board obligations.

STAFFING

The Family House has 10 full-time employees. They include an executive director, a day and a night manager, two clinical supervisors, and 5 social workers or counselors who provide direct services to families. Social workers are assigned to specific families and provide the aftercare services to the assigned family upon exit from the House. The two clinical managers also handle direct services approximately 30% of the time; the rest of their time is spent handling group sessions and overseeing the direct services offered by the social workers. The House managers supervise the facility and maintain the grounds, take referrals over the phone, assist families with check-in, establish housekeeping obligations, and supervise the volunteer program. The executive director oversees all functions of the House, staffs the Board of Directors (including fund raising, speaking engagements, finance, and house operations), prepares budget materials and grant and funding applications, supervises staff, and interacts with the community to encourage referrals and receive community responses to the program. The executive director maintains statistics of client services and advocates, as needed, throughout the community for the needs associated with the client population.

The response of staff to the assessment questionnaire indicated they feel that the supervision of staff and volunteers is generally good. The House managers feel they have difficulty completing tasks in a timely fashion, partially as a result of the large fluctuation of client population and partially as a result of difficulty in time management. The service delivery is of an extremely high quality, and employee retention levels are high.

The staff needs the following resources: (1) salaries that are comparable to those in other organizations; (2) sufficient office space for administrative needs and sufficient privacy available for client counseling when the House is full; (3) more in-service training to keep staff professionally challenged; and (4) training in supervision skills and time management for managers. One additional area that requires attention is the delineation of roles and responsibilities between staffmembers and volunteers.

VOLUNTEERS

The Family House volunteer program has approximately 100 members. The average length of involvement with the House is 2 years. Most of the volunteers contact the agency to become involved; very little active recruitment is done. Currently, this does not pose a problem, but as the agency ages and becomes less novel, it may need to institute an active recruitment program.

Volunteers assist with House maintenance; help with recreational activities for House residents; offer travel assistance to work, school, and doctor appointments; and provide respite services to children or siblings, thereby allowing parents the time to address their own adult needs. According to the responses received from interviews and questionnaires, the volunteers are quite enthusiastic about their assignments, but they tend to try to offer counseling services rather than performing their assigned tasks. This is the primary area in which staff and volunteer roles tend to become blurred. Volunteers are good about adhering to their schedules and have recently begun their own fund raising efforts, which have increased their involvement with the House.

Resources needed for the volunteer program include scheduled training sessions on a semiannual basis and some type of recognition to honor those who devote their time and energy to our program. The Board tends to be less interested in the volunteer program than in other Board committees. The addition of the volunteer committee chair to the Executive Committee would provide a greater awareness and appreciation for the program among the Board members. Within the next year, the program size needs to be closely monitored to determine if it is necessary to begin an active recruitment program.

FACILITIES AND EQUIPMENT

Additional office space is needed for administrative staff, clinical services, Board members, and volunteers. The House has sufficient space for families yet insufficient space for the intervention and support services required to keep the program successful.

The House budget needs to reflect a willingness to invest in quality equipment and computer software. Both staff and volunteer surveys indicate that too much time is spent trying to secure donations of used equipment or personally designed software programs. As a result, the equipment and software are difficult to maintain and much time is lost changing systems and equipment as we are always searching for something that will actually meet our growing needs.

The House has recently been redecorated and painted, so for the next several years we should have no major expenses related to maintaining the family living areas.

ORGANIZATIONAL STRUCTURE

Two areas of confusion currently exist within the Family House: responsibilities between staff and Board members and staff and volunteers. An organizational chart and updated job descriptions for all parties need to be created. The growth of the program has resulted in changes without a corresponding change in written descriptions of tasks and responsibilities. The Volunteer Chair needs to have a higher profile within the Board; placing the Chair on the Executive Committee would allow greater recognition.

FINANCIAL OVERVIEW

Essentially, the House has operated well within its budget, and a base of annual donors has been established through a Friends campaign.

The House has successfully retired two of its three mortgages and has an outstanding note of approximately $50,000.

State funding may be less secure based upon recent state financial problems, and the $75,000 grant may be reduced in the future. The Board needs to begin planning on a revenue source to replace this base source of income.

Family House Internal Assessment Summary

Discussion: The information contained within the internal assessment is lengthy and will be difficult to use at a later date when the material is to be synthesized for use at the board's retreat and for preparing the draft strategic plan. Therefore, the information is summarized in Tables 3.7 and 3.8 for use later in the planning process.

Table 3.7 Family House Internal Assessment Summary

Internal Assessment Summary — DRAFT

The Strategic Planning Committee has completed the Internal Assessment, and the following issues have been raised:

1. Board of Directors: Lack of a clear direction for the Board, coupled with the absence of any Board leadership development program, was the greatest concern expressed by Board members. Board members are unclear about future direction of the House.

2. Staff: Primary area of concern was the need for resources to increase salary levels and provide professional development. Staffmembers have many ideas about future of House but are unclear about how to present these to the Board.

3. Volunteers: We need a clear delineation of volunteer and staff roles and greater recognition from the Board regarding the contributions of the volunteers.

4. Facilities and equipment: We have a general need for more space and equipment to support the services of the House; the Board needs a workstation at the House, and staffmembers need an additional private area for clinical work and more administrative space.

Table 3.8. Family House Internal Assessment Summary Table

Resources	Performance	Process
• Staff salary levels • additional space and equipment	• Lack of space for clinical services affects quality of services • Lack of space for Board affects its leadership role in organization	• Board leadership development • Board clarity on House's future • Volunteer and staff roles overlap • Staff lacks formal system for presenting ideas to the Board

Community College Foundation: Internal Assessment

EXECUTIVE SUMMARY

In December, the Strategic Planning Committee of the Community College Foundation adopted a planning process for composing the strategic plan. The first phase of this planning process consisted of structured interviews of all Foundation Board members and Emeritus Board members. The interview instrument was approved at the January meeting of the Committee.

Foundation Mission

The overwhelming majority of the Board responded consistently to the Foundation's mission statement, which reflected the following themes:

1. to raise funds,
2. to support the Community College's goals, and
3. to manage the Foundation's assets.

A few respondents had an unclear sense of the mission, primarily because of a feeling that the Foundation was fragmented in its direction.

Mission Effectiveness

The Board's feeling on mission effectiveness is diverse. With respect to the fund raising portion of the mission, there seems to be an evenly divided opinion. Several Board members have expressed admiration at the amount of funds raised in recent years, while others believe that the Foundation has not done particularly well.

There was almost universal agreement that the Foundation has not done an adequate job in promoting the Community College to the community.

Very little opinion was expressed regarding the impact the Foundation has had upon the Community College, and a few respondents felt that the stewardship of Foundation assets has been acceptable.

Foundation Strengths

The major strengths of the Community College Foundation, as identified by the Board members, can be categorized as follows:

1. the quality, diversity, and potential of the Board members;
2. the growing credibility and quality of the Community College;
3. the vision and leadership of the new President; and
4. the Foundation's growing financial strength.

Areas for Improvement

The major weaknesses, commonly identified by the Board members, are as follows:

1. lack of vision and focus for the Foundation;
2. weak participation by Board members;
3. poor community visibility for the Foundation; and
4. no sense of cohesiveness on the part of the Board.

Areas of Opportunity During the Next Five Years

The areas most frequently identified as opportunities for the Foundation in the next 5 years are listed as follows:

1. building relationships with the community that will lead to gift income;
2. instituting a program to involve and solicit alumni;
3. using the emergence of the new President as a community leader to create opportunities;
4. seeking real estate and planned gift opportunities; and
5. developing the Board into a more active organization.

Board member responses to this section of the survey tend to reflect strategic directions rather than a solid definition of opportunities for the Foundation.

Community College and Foundation Relationship

The overall consensus of the Board is that it wishes to have a close working relationship with the Community College while maintaining its independence. Although most of the responses to this survey issue were not specific in actually defining a working relationship between the two entities, Board members were able to articulate elements or characteristics of a satisfactory relationship.

In the aggregate, these elements suggest the following as a framework for mutually supporting roles between the Community College and the Foundation:

1. The Foundation Board wishes to be responsive to the leadership of the Community College President in pursuing the highest priorities for fostering excellence at the Community College. The Board feels strongly about having the new President as a presence in the Foundation.
2. The Foundation Board is looking to the Community College to become more aggressive in its communications with the community so as to permit the Foundation, in its supporting role, to better take advantage of the stature of the Community College.
3. The Foundation Board wishes to be looked upon as a major player in the Community College's future development.

Community College Support Groups and the Foundation

Approximately 50% of the interviewed Board members believed that some sort of formal cooperative relationship should exist between the Foundation and various other Community College fund raising support groups. This relationship, it was felt, should be based mostly on coordination of activities and fund raising rather than on the Foundation taking over control of these other operations.

It was also suggested that there be a mechanism to bring the best of these support group members to the Foundation as future Board members.

Community College Foundation Board Member Roles

A strong desire clearly exists among the Board members to become more active in the Foundation, but no clear consensus exists on what forms or levels of participation are best. Several Board members felt that no common understanding exists among Board members as to what may constitute active membership and support of the Foundation mission.

The following is a listing of roles suggested as appropriate for Board members:

1. Be an advocate and a knowledgeable supporter.
2. Make a gift to the Foundation.
3. Help raise funds for the Foundation.
4. Attend meetings regularly.
5. Get involved with an area of the Community College.
6. Do public relations work for the Community College.
7. Do committee work.
8. Recruit new talent to the Foundation Board and the Community College.

Several Board members suggested that it would be most appropriate first to determine what we want the Foundation to be as an organization and then to determine what roles are most appropriate for fulfilling that mission.

The Setting of Priorities

Each Board member was asked to imagine beginning the Foundation from scratch in 199x and to set priorities for the organization. This is a method of focusing the Board on the task of setting priorities.

The most frequent responses to this question are as follows:

1. determine the Community College's needs;
2. draft a mission statement;
3. recruit a strong, dedicated Board willing to act (include as many prominent Community College graduates as possible);

4. develop a plan of action to meet the needs of the Community College;
5. hire a professional staff; and
6. involve the President of the Community College in carrying out the mission.

It is interesting that the Board member responses to this question focused primarily on the process of doing things rather than on the product or results of that process. This may be a reflection of the manner in which the question was posed, or perhaps it could represent a mode of thinking that presently guides the functioning of the Board.

Community College Foundation Goals for 199x

Many Foundation Board members had difficulty in expressing specific types of goals that should be achieved in the next 5 years. Much of this difficulty has its roots in a general lack of understanding of the Community College's goals and needs as expressed previously in this report. Generally, however, the Board's responses can be summarized as follows:

1. Dramatically increase the endowment funds of the Foundation.
2. Generate a vibrant esprit de corps among the Board or rebuild the Board.
3. Have dramatic and exciting projects to work on originating from the President of the Community College.
4. Play the leading role in the next Community College fund drive.
5. Establish a program of effective communication with the community on behalf of the Community College.

Other Strategic Planning Issues

The Board members offered numerous suggestions for issues needing attention by the Committee in the planning process. The following list summarizes these concerns:

1. Board member involvement could be strengthened by improving the participatory format of the Board meetings, holding meetings on the campus, increasing the familiarity among the members, and better recognizing the service of its past and present members.
2. Board members generally desire an improved program of Board education that features regular presentations from the Community College faculty and key administrative staff.
3. The Board senses a significant presence of untapped wealth in the community but feels the need for a sharper delineation of the Community College's needs before this wealth can be directed to the Foundation.
4. The Board feels that the community lacks a close association with the Community College.

5. Several Board members believe that another Private College Foundation has been better able to project a presence in the local community.

Discussion

Some general indications of this portion of the strategic planning process for the Community College Foundation are as follows:

1. *Mission.* Although the Board members seemed to have a consensus opinion of the Foundation mission elements, there is a divergence of opinion regarding the effectiveness of the Foundation in pursuing its mission.

2. *Ownership.* The Board members generally desire greater ownership and involvement in the Foundation. This stems from the lack of clearly defined goals and objectives for the Foundation, as well as uncertainty regarding the roles Board members should be playing.

3. *Communication.* Generally, Board members feel uninformed regarding the Community College's goals, programs, and needs.

4. *Visibility.* There is a consensus among the Board that the Foundation's visibility is fairly weak in the community and among potential donors. This is related generally to the positioning of the Community College overall in the community. There has been high praise, however, for the new President in opening the line of communication and understanding between the Community College and the community.

5. *Potential.* Most Board members believe that there is enormous but untapped potential within the present Board.

Community College Foundation Internal Assessment Summary

Once again, the lengthy internal assessment has been summarized to allow for ease of use while you prepare for the Board retreat and the draft strategic planning report. Tables 3.9 and 3.10 summarize the information for the Community College Foundation.

Table 3.9 Foundation Internal Assessment Summary

Community College Foundation Internal Assessment Summary
The Strategic Planning Committee has completed the Internal Assessment, and
the following themes were noted in the course of our work:

1. We found almost universal agreement that the Foundation has not adequately promoted the Community College to the community.

2. The Foundation Board wishes to be looked upon as a major player in the Community College's future development.

3. The Board members believe that an enormous potential within the present Board remains untapped.

Table 3.10 Foundation Internal Assessment Summary Chart

Resources	Performance	Process
• Untapped potential of current Board members	• Inadequate promotion of the Community College to the community	• Foundation lacks prestige or influence within the Community College itself

4

External Assessment

A nonprofit organization may have a worthy mission, capable staff, volunteers, and a committed board of directors, but these positive attributes will go unnoticed if its services are not readily used by the target client population. A "marketing orientation" is as vital a perspective to nonprofits as it is to businesses.

The purpose of the external assessment is to gather information from the community and determine how well your organization is responding to the identified needs that your organization was created to address. All nonprofit organizations are formed to address an identified need or condition that affects a specific population. Whether the organization provides services or resources for that specific population, the original premise for the nonprofit's creation is to respond to a need or condition that, for whatever reason, lacks existing resources or attention.

Perhaps no other part of the strategic planning process is as vital to the nonprofit organization's long-term success as the external assessment. If the external assessment is accomplished openly, objectively, and thoroughly, it will provide a well-crafted vision of the marketplace and the environmental factors that affect the organization. If the external assessment, however, is handled from a defensive, predisposed posture, then the result will have little value to the organization or the planning process.

Based on external perceptions and changes in the identified needs of the population or the wider community, several examples of required organizational changes help to illustrate the vital need for the external assessment.

Over time, the original identified need addressed by the organization may be satisfied, as seen, for example, in the March of Dimes efforts to combat polio and the development of the polio vaccine. The original identified need was seemingly satisfied. The March of Dimes then decided to focus on continuing its successful work in a wider area of need that included low-birth-weight babies and resultant birth defects.

In other instances, the identified need may have altered over time because of changes in the surrounding community or a lack of sufficient resources to maintain an effort that has lost its significance for the target population. In the early 1980s, single-sex youth-enrichment programs became controversial in many communities. Although the Girl Scouts and Boy Scouts for the most part retained their single-sex orientation, Campfire, previously an all-girl program, expanded to include boys. Numerous local athletic programs found themselves grappling with the issue of allowing girls to participate in previously all-boy programs. These changes were handled differently by different organizations, but the primary motivation was a change in the interests of the target population and the marketplace.

Throughout the 1980s, hospitals experienced similar shifts in their service delivery options. With changes in the regulatory and reimbursement policies of government and private entities, hospitals changed their primary emphasis from acute care to services that include outpatient care, home health care, and preferred-provider agreements.

These organizations were required to revisit their missions and activities and determine what changes were required to continue their vital work. Nonprofits function in the same rapidly changing environment that affects all of our lives. We would err in assuming that changes, which affect so many aspects of our daily personal and work lives, will not also affect the work of nonprofits in some way.

The basic components of the external assessment include interviews and input from external stakeholders, market conditions and community interests and needs, regulatory and legal environments, and assessments of the resource base.

External Stakeholders

Like the preceding internal assessment, the external assessment involves assessing both the perceptions and facts related to the work of your organization. The external assessment involves interviewing key external stakeholders in a similar fashion as the previous work with internal stakeholders.

External stakeholders include the following:

- clients or recipients;
- funding sources;
- referral or cooperative organizations;
- organizations that serve the same population or seek resources from the same sources; and
- community leaders from business, civic, and private organizations.

These stakeholders will tell different stories about the work of your organization, based on a variety of factors, including their direct interactions with your organization, the information they have learned from other sources about your organization, and their own perceptions about the changing needs of the community in which they live.

Market Conditions

Historically, nonprofit organizations have not fully addressed the range of issues that profit-oriented organizations must embrace in terms of marketing. For business, the "four P's" of successful marketing—product, place, promotion, and price—are critical. These concepts are important tools for nonprofit organizations to understand and include in their external assessments.

In terms of this workbook, *product* includes the services or resources that your nonprofit provides to the community. Included in the discussion of your organizational product are such issues as uniqueness, comprehensiveness, ancillary services, and affiliations with national or local entities.

Place refers to the actual location of services such as the central office and any outreach facilities. The accessibility of the services or resources your organization offers may have an enormous effect on whether the services or resources are used by the target population. For this workbook, *place* also refers to the system of referrals that actively bring clients to your organization.

For nonprofit organizations, *promotion* includes the agency's focused public relations and fund raising efforts as well as broader efforts involved with raising public awareness about the issues that affect your target population or its associated needs.

Price concerns not only the actual fees collected as part of the service or resource delivery, but also any regulatory influences that may affect sliding-fee scales or even the authority to collect fees. If your organization is limited in its ability to charge fees, then the price associated with the delivery of services or resources will still need to be addressed. This price factor may then become a key motivating issue for future fund raising.

To be financially successful, businesses must strategically organize the marketing mix of the four P's. Nonprofit organizations must also find the appropriate mix that allows the organization to effectively deliver its services or resources. The four P's require attention in the strategic planning process, especially when the external assessment is being conducted. The four P's may seem to remain constant over time, yet rarely is that the case. The needs and attitudes of the target population may change, the community's response to these issues may change and produce other organizations that may benefit from novelty or increased exposure, or variables in the marketplace as a whole may change. Thus, all of the previously believed information may change in some unanticipated fashion.

Market Assessment

The external assessment provides a vehicle for you to evaluate your organization in relationship to the "market" that comprises your community, referring and funding entities, and client population. The first question to be addressed is, "Who are we serving and what are their needs?" To answer this question, the strategic planning committee will need to collect demographic indicators that help to define the population being served.

These demographic indicators can be obtained from federal, state, or local studies. Such resources indicate the prevalence of the condition that your agency addresses or the prevalence of accompanying needs that indicate a high probability that the services or resources will be needed. Table 4.1 lists many of these sources of demographic information.

Table 4.1 Potential Sources of Demographic Information

- Federal, state, county or municipal agencies: Reports in such areas as human resources, revenue reports, mental health, health care, and population statistics, including income levels and size of households.
- United Way and community councils: Reports on services and needs in your community.
- Information and referral networks: Data on need for services.
- Annual reports for major private foundations in your community.
- Periodicals and journals of the professional organizations that are involved in your organization's area of expertise.
- Newspapers, local and national, that discuss the needs of your target population.
- Police departments: Sometimes information is available on specific crime rates in target neighborhoods.
- School systems, health care institutions, and other organizations that serve a corollary need for your target population.
- Planning councils connected with either the local government or a local university.

For example, if the federal census reports that 20% of the local population is at or below the poverty level and other reports indicate that 90% of families at or below the poverty level are single-parent families, then you may be able to make the case that services for latch-key children are needed by approximately 20% of the local population. In this isolated example of demographics, you would then determine what 20% of the local population is in terms of client numbers. The result then would be compared to the actual number of clients you have served over the past one or two years. You now have some idea about how many of the potential clients are actually receiving your agency's services.

Once you have quantified the client base, you need to determine how much of this population is actually being reached by your organization. If you are only reaching one quarter of the population, then what is the reason? Are you unable to provide more services or are you unable to reach more clients? In many ways, the answer to both questions involves gaining knowledge about your *competition*. Although the term may seem to be an odd one for a nonprofit to use, in a very real sense you are competing for philanthropic and volunteer support, even if you maintain a cooperative relationship on a service level.

If you have a long waiting list, then justifying your organization's services is easy. Sadly, a waiting list is a frustrating experience for clients, especially if the service being offered is vital to their well-being. Your mission is to serve this population. Even if you cannot offer them services directly, your mission implies that you are willing to provide some type of referral or temporary measure. Therefore, it becomes important for you to know about similar services or organizations available in your community.

If you are having difficulty reaching clients, you also need to know about other services these clients might be using. If the services are similar to your own, then you need to find out why clients are choosing the other agency.

- Does the other agency offer more support services? a wider array of services?
- Are the other services easier to access?
- Do they cost less or require less of the client?
- If another agency has a reputation for competency in certain areas, does this allow your agency to express its services in another fashion?
- What is unique about your services? Does that uniqueness have value to your client?
- How can you translate your commitment (and your mission) into a valuable service to your client?

In some instances, you may need to determine how a client knows that he or she needs the service or resource. An individual who is homeless may have the concrete realization that he or she needs a home. But a person also might have so many **accompanying needs** that he or she may not see housing as the most pressing need at the moment. The client may be more focused on finding employment, food, or medical care.

Frequently, underlying "value" statements accompany social services. If these values are opposed to other aspects of the individual's life-style, the potential client may avoid the offered services. Your organization must clearly understand the implied values and the conflicting issues that receiving services or resources may entail.

For example, a local Girl Scout Council established a priority of offering services to a neighborhood that was composed primarily of immigrant families. The families were asked about their interest in the Girl Scouts and indicated that they had positive views of the services. However, once the traditional Girl Scout program was established, very few girls arrived to participate. The council returned to the parents to identify the perceived problem. The parents stated that they all worked during the day and were fearful of the potentially "bad" influences in the neighborhood that might affect their daughters. They had all given their daughters strict instructions to return home directly from school and to avoid leaving home until their parents returned at the end of the day. At this point, the council needed to change the program substantially if it wished to serve these girls. The program began on weekend afternoons when parents could attend with their daughters and observe directly what types of activities were occurring. Over time, as the families became more comfortable with the program, the council was able to shift the program to include activities after school. The fundamental error that led to poor participation was a failure to understand a key life-style issue in the target population.

If your client population is reluctant to acknowledge the need for your services, what types of referral systems might increase acceptance? Referrals are important, not only to maintain your client base, but also to indicate community support for your organization. If the Girl Scout program had not worked on weekends and the council still wished to offer services, then it might have decided to co-sponsor activities with a neighborhood organization that was already trusted and accepted by the community, such as a local church.

Do any associated needs accompany your identified need? Perhaps these associated needs will attract clients more readily and allow you to provide your own in-house referrals. Perhaps you need to offer an auxiliary service to attract clients. For example, a child-development agency wishing to offer parent-training programs may need to provide child care during the program. The lack of child care may prevent parents from attending an important program that would offer them needed skills and information. If child care were available, they would be quite willing to attend. In fact, they might be willing to pay for the service, thereby allowing the agency to benefit in several ways while providing a valuable client service.

As you compared your organization's services with those of similar local organizations, did you notice any program ideas that would be desirable to initiate? Did you uncover unmet needs? These represent possible new programs or opportunities for your strategic plan.

Determining whether an unmet need exists because of a lack of attention or a specific reason is important. Some unmet needs remain unmet because offering the service is financially infeasible. It is important to evaluate potential obstacles that may arise with a new program that is designed to address unmet needs.

Regulatory and Legal Environments

Depending on the service or resource that your nonprofit provides, you may be subject to regulatory or legal environments that may change over time. If you have a site where services are provided, the organization may be required to have permits or licenses and may be subject to inspection by any number of state or local authorities. These inspections or codes may require the organization to modify or alter some aspects of the facilities over time as laws change or facilities age.

Recently, many communities and states have begun to impose statutes governing fund raising efforts. In some communities, the nonprofit must receive a fund raising permit to conduct special events or even fund raising mailings. These permits may require the nonprofit to present the city council with the planned year's activities as well as recently performed audits. Generally, as communities grow and receive increases in appeals for funding, they may wish to evaluate these activities and protect themselves from potentially unscrupulous activities.

If the nonprofit receives funding from federal or state entities, the laws governing these entities may affect the nonprofit's work. The funding requirements may include regular reports or site visits as well as maintaining records on types of services provided in conjunction with the funding provided.

Essentially, the regulatory and legal environments require attention while the strategic plan is being created, because any changes may affect the costs associated with the provision of resources or services. If, in the course of the external assessment, the strategic planning committee learns that funding may be available from a new source, then the "strings" attached to the funding must be evaluated for their effects on the total organization. These strings are the regulatory or legal requirements that may accompany the desired funding.

5

External Assessment Tools and Instruments

Survey and Interview Techniques

Depending on the size of the community in which your organization functions, the external stakeholders may represent a fairly large group of people. For those individuals and groups with whom your organization has funding or direct referral relationships, the external assessment is best conducted by using personal interviews. These interviews are quite similar in nature to the internal assessment interviews that were previously discussed.

The strategic planning committee will want to contact both staff and volunteer leaders of the funding and referral organizations for interviews. The staff may provide a picture most closely related to the actual working arrangements between your organizations, while the volunteer leaders will have more information on the ways in which both of the organizational goals may or may not coincide and general trends in the community of which the other organizations are aware.

Once again, these interviews should not be used as opportunities to challenge the beliefs and opinions of external stakeholders. This is the time to listen and discuss the perceptions that are being shared (see Table 5.1).

Table 5.1 Sample External Stakeholder Interview Instrument

1. How did you first become aware of our organization?
2. What do you believe is our organization's mission?
3. How effective is our organization in meeting or addressing the existing needs of our community?
4. What types of community changes should our organization consider as we engage in strategic planning? Does our community have unmet needs that we should be addressing?
5. How well do our separate organizations work together in serving the community? Are you aware of any areas that require attention on our part?
6. What types of future plans are you presently making for your organization?
7. Do you feel our organization is providing an important service to the community? If not, why not?
8. What suggestions do you have for us as we conduct this strategic planning exercise?

Survey Techniques for External Stakeholders

The external assessment can be conducted in several ways, but the methods you choose should reflect the strategic planning committee's goals to involve the community in your organization. As mentioned previously, for those external stakeholders who have funding, regulatory, or referral relationships with your organization, the ideal assessment procedure is the personal interview.

These specific external stakeholders are vital to your organization's continued existence: They provide funds, regulate your services, or provide clients. The personal interview format will allow the committee to create personal contacts that may be valuable for the organization over time. This is not meant to be an attempt to curry favor with these stakeholders. It is meant to open a dialogue with stakeholders who play a key role in your organization's continued functioning.

Former and current clients probably are more appropriately asked to complete a brief questionnaire that can be delivered by mail or given in person or by telephone. Depending on the nature of the service or resources you provide, client confidentiality may be an issue. If so, you can create a questionnaire that does not ask for the client's name and that includes a preprinted, stamped envelope for return. Although written questionnaires may be difficult to collect, clients generally can be asked to respond while they are at the agency, and the retrieval rate is much higher.

In specific, you need to learn about any barriers that exist from the client's perspective. These barriers may include access to services, eligibility for services, the agency's location, costs of service, and delivery speed or waiting time associated with the service. Depending on the services or resources that your organization provides, you may also need to ask about any physical barriers at the organization that prevent access to services or any language or cultural barriers that limit clients' access to your organization's services or resources (see Table 5.2).

Constituent Sampling Techniques

The remaining external stakeholders include business and civic leaders as well as individuals and groups who are involved in serving the same or similar populations that are served by your agency. Conducting personal interviews with such a large group may not be feasible for the strategic planning committee. Instead, the committee might convene focus groups and invite 10 to 15 individuals from a wide variety of backgrounds to participate in a structured meeting.

For example, if the Family House wished to determine how well it was serving the community and what types of changes might occur in the future to affect its services, it could convene a focus group of professionals involved with the same client group, civic leaders working in the community, and representatives from other organizations serving similar client groups. The format for the group would be to openly discuss, with the help of a facilitator, the issues raised by two questions: (1) How well does Family House serve the community? (2) What changes in the community will require changes in Family House's services?

Formats for Constituent Sampling

Constituent sampling can occur through focus groups, mini-retreats, or brainstorming sessions. These exercises all share the common purpose of bringing together individuals and allowing thoughtful discussion and review of a focal point of relevance to the organization that has called for the meeting.

The focus group can range in size from 2 to 15 participants. The size of the group will determine the need for one or more facilitators,

Table 5.2 Sample Client Interview Instrument

1. How did you first learn of our agency?
2. How long have you been using our agency's services?
3. How easy or difficult has it been to receive services at our agency?
4. Does our location make it easy or difficult for you to come in?
5. Have our fees been appropriate? Why or why not?
6. Has the staff responded quickly to your requests? Do you have to wait a long time for help?
7. Has our organization helped you? How?
8. Can we do anything to be more helpful to you?
9. As we plan for the future, do you have any advice for us?

recorders, or assistants to ensure that the agenda for the meeting is followed and time is well spent. The meeting area should allow the participants to be comfortable throughout the planned duration of the meeting. Generally, the meeting should not be longer than several hours; constituent interests in your organization's needs dwindle with longer periods of time.

Before the meeting, the agenda and any materials that will be presented should be mailed to participants to allow preparation for the meeting and to encourage anticipation for the activity. The agenda should also note a phone number where messages can be left for participants should such a need arise. Refreshments should be offered, and the agenda should include breaks to permit participants to remain alert.

The facilitator's job is to keep the group focused and monitor time. The facilitator also must work to ensure that all of the participants actually participate. Some quite enthusiastic participants may need to be curbed so that less vocal members can become more actively involved.

The individual who records the meeting can record the ideas generated on large pads to allow participants to see the issues as they talk. Another option is to record the meeting and then later send minutes of the meeting to the participants. In this fashion, any new ideas or issues that are raised in the course of the meeting can be shared with others who also may have a compelling interest to address some of these issues.

Another option is to convene a focus group with several members from the same organization and conduct the meeting at their location. For example, a hospital meeting might include representatives from social services, nursing, physicians, public relations, and appropriate individuals within the hospital who interact with either the agency itself or its clients.

Synthesizing the External Stakeholder Assessments

Once you have completed the interviews, questionnaires, or focus groups, the information will need to be synthesized so that it may be analyzed and discussions about necessary changes can be initiated.

These interviews and questionnaires may provide more anecdotal than concrete information. The strategic planning committee will want to sift through the responses and determine whether any clear messages are received from a variety of sources. One example might be the question of mission: Is this information clearly agreed upon or do different individuals have different perceptions about the mission of your organization?

Ideally, the strategic planning committee will want to create a list of areas in which disagreement or lack of consensus indicates that further attention is warranted. If the committee believes that external stakeholders hold opinions that sharply disagree with those held by internal stakeholders, then these also will require further attention.

The two draft summary reports and market assessments for the Family House and the Community College Foundation are shown in Tables 5.5, 5.6, 5.7, and 5.8; they were created during the committees' first passes at the external stakeholder assessments. Once the other components of the external assessment have been completed, these reports will require revision to determine whether key information was overlooked in the first passes.

Assessing the Resource Base

A nonprofit organization's resource base includes all sources of funding, both cash and in-kind support. The financial assessment in Chapter 4 delineated the types of funding currently received by the organization. These may include fees, donations, and special events and fund raising efforts. For the external assessment, analyzing your organizational efforts according to program (or purpose) and analyzing the types of resources that support these efforts are more helpful approaches.

The Family House provides family activities as part of its overall program. The family activities program is comprehensive and seeks to provide outlets for the families to engage in a variety of activities, including art, sports, reading programs, field trips, cooking, and science activities. The program is administered by the staff, but the activities are conducted by volunteers. The resource base for the family activities program is varied and highly dependent on the specific component of the program that most interests the donors. A local art merchants group contributes supplies (in-kind donation), while a corporate foundation provides $1,500 annually to the program for use as needed. Perhaps the most interesting factor about the family activities program is that these donations are received without a concerted fund raising effort on the part of the Family House. The Family House will need to review the past donations and determine which ones were specifically targeted for the family activities program. The program's resource base is shown in Table 5.3.

The Community College Foundation has a small program that provides mentors for minority students. The program requires relatively little cash but depends heavily on the volunteers to schedule time with their students and to provide necessary support and guidance. Twice a year, the program holds an event that gathers all of the students and mentors together. The resource base for the program is shown in Table 5.4.

Writing the External Assessment

The completed external assessment should provide information that is relevant and useful to the target audience. At this point in the process, your target audience is primarily the board of directors and any internal stakeholders, such as key staff, who may have a role in the upcoming retreat and the formulation of the completed plan.

The two examples that follow use different formats to convey their messages. The Family House has presented its external assessment by type of stakeholder. The Community College Foundation has presented its information by theme. The stylistic differences show the direction in which these fictional organizations are going. For your purposes, you may wish to shape the results of the external assessment to be more readily usable for the priority setting and the identification of opportunities that will be covered in the next chapter.

Family House External Assessment

As part of the overall strategic planning process, a series of interviews and focus groups were conducted with members of the

Table 5.3 Family House Resource Base for Activities Program

Contributions		
Donor	**Cash ($)**	**In-kind ($ value)**
ABC Corporation	1,500	
Art Merchants		500 (art supplies)
Sport Team	500	500 (tickets)
Science Corporation	500	
Milk Company		350 (food)
Grocery Store		1,000 (food)

general community, donors, referral sources, state agencies, and clients. The results of these interviews are summarized and provide helpful and insightful information about external stakeholders' perceptions of the Family House.

CLIENTS

Family House clients are interviewed three times during their stay at the House: upon admission, midway through their stay, and upon exit. These client interviews were used to gather information for the external assessment. Generally, women value the Family House services more initially than do men. Both view referral to the House has a "final option" prior to court-ordered separation. Upon admission, men tend to feel themselves as the identified family problem and feel uncomfortable with this assumption.

The physical facilities available for clients are viewed as comfortable and appropriate. The respite care program is the service most identified as specifically helpful for parents. There have been requests to have more male staff to facilitate the clinical sessions. The aftercare program is considered to be highly effective. Some clients have expressed an interest to serve as volunteers or "mentors" for new families entering the House.

REFERRAL SOURCES

Referral sources are generally quite enthusiastic about the Family House. Three issues were raised, however, that may require more attention.

1. The community need for this service far exceeds the capacity of Family House. Referral sources question whether the House program is too long, thereby limiting needlessly the number of families who can be served. Referral sources would prefer a shorter stay at the House with a longer aftercare program.

Table 5.4 Community College Foundation's Mentor Program Resource Base

Contributions		
Donor	**Cash ($)**	**In-kind ($ value)**
Associated Students		250 (meeting room)
Black Women	500	
Professionals		
Hispanic Coalition		500 (food, one event)
Retired Teachers	250	
Newspaper	300	500 (food, one event)
Fraternal Organization		150 (recognition)

2. Cultural sensitivity has been raised as an issue. The Family House is not perceived as providing a culturally diverse context for the intervention services offered.

3. Some Family House clients seem to become more dependent over time, thus making their return to independent living more difficult. These clients have difficulty leaving the structure and support offered at the House.

DONORS

Donors feel pleased with the work of the House and believe their contributions are valued and effective in addressing a pressing community need. A growing number of former clients have become donors to the House.

STATE AGENCIES

The agencies represent both referral sources and funding sources in their relationship to the House. They are quite pleased with the program but feel that too few clients are served, based on the growing need for successful intervention in abusive families.

COMMUNITY LEADERS

The Family House is well respected in the community because of the success of the clinical intervention. Once again, the primary issues raised were: Why does the treatment last so long and why are so few families able to participate?

The Family House interacts with a substantial number of regulatory entities including law enforcement and the courts, zoning and licensing for group home, health code for food service, and building safety codes. The House is in full compliance with all of these entities' requirements.

Table 5.5 Summary Report for Family House

Family House External Stakeholder Assessment — DRAFT

The interviews and questionnaires have all been completed and the Strategic Planning Committee has noted the following issues:

1. Our mission is not clearly delineated to the community as a whole. The mission was most frequently described as "temporary assistance in domestic violence cases."

2. The increasing incidence of domestic violence in the community has prompted many respondents to wonder why we serve only 15 to 20 families at a time and why the length of stay is so long.

3. Clients who have been involved with the House for longer than 1 month speak quite highly of the value of the services. New clients are more likely to be equivocal in their responses.

Table 5.6 Market Assessment for Family House

Price	**Product**
• Insurance companies	• Respite care
	• Male staff
	• Client dependency
Place (demand and access)	**Promotion**
• Shorter house program	• Cultural diversity
• Longer aftercare	• Perception

The Family House has a resource base composed of four distinct sources: fund raising, insurance, state grants, and client fees. The issues raised regarding resources focus on developing new resources and establishing greater ties with existing funding sources. Assessing the feasibility of increasing agency fund raising to compensate for declining state funding and a possible erosion of client fee base as well as increasing communication with insurance and state funding sources may adequately solve these issues.

Community College Foundation External Assessment

The external assessment for the Community College Foundation consisted of 20 interviews with business, corporate, and community leaders; past Board members; major donors; and faculty and students. The strategic planning committee was primarily interested in perceptions about the Community College and about the Foundation. The following three trends were noted by representatives from all of the external stakeholder constituencies.

First, the Community College Foundation is not clearly differentiated from the other support groups on campus. Other support groups have developed core groups of supporters who have a better understanding of what they are being asked to do for the Community College. These support groups frequently compete with each other for the attention of key community leaders and donors. The absence of a centralized vehicle for minimizing competition among the groups was viewed as a problem for major donors.

Second, the Community College Foundation has maintained a low profile with the projects and funds it has supervised. The Foundation's work is neither well understood nor highly valued by any of the individuals interviewed. Everyone commented on the great potential that exists but which remains untapped.

Third, the Community College and the Foundation are not well represented in the general community. The historically low profile has caused the community to feel less than supportive about the work of the Community College and the Foundation. The enrollment growth in the past decade has prompted many students and faculty to fear a decrease in quality. Although the corporate community is quite positive about the Community College's work, the rest of the community lacks an appreciation for the vital role it plays in extended education opportunities for employees of major corporations.

The following regulatory and legal issues face the Community College Foundation:

1. If the Foundation were autonomous, the Community College might have more flexibility with the funds raised by the Foundation.
2. Currently, it is difficult maintaining the privacy of donor records and confidentiality for major donors.
3. The state solicitation statutes are currently under scrutiny by the Legislature and may require changes in operating procedures for the Foundation.

The Community College Foundation resource base is limited and highly focused. The multiple support groups on campus and the ensuing competition for donors has not helped the Foundation. Corporate and private support have been moderate. The community as a whole is viewed as having considerable wealth and the potential for substantial support for future Community College and Foundation projects.

Table 5.7 Summary Report for Community College Foundation

Community College Foundation External Stakeholder Assessment — DRAFT
We have just completed our interview of the key external stakeholders, and the following issues require further discussion:

1. External stakeholders had difficulty differentiating our Foundation from the numerous other support groups on campus.

2. The use of the funds raised by the Foundation was not viewed as critical by a variety of groups whose members do not feel adequately represented on the campus, whether staff, professors, or students.

3. Clearly, community leaders see a leadership vacuum in terms of who best represents the Community College to the community.

Table 5.8 Market Assessment for Community College Foundation

Price	Product
	• Untapped potential
	• Donor record confidentiality
Place	**Promotion**
• Autonomy	• Similarity to other support groups
	• Low profile

6

Identifying Key Issues and Targeting Opportunities

Assessing Key Issues

In the preceding chapters, the strategic planning process has investigated the perceptions of current operations and suggestions for future change from both the internal and external stakeholders. These assessments now need to be synthesized and key issues identified so that the organization can evaluate any target opportunities that it chooses to address.

The target opportunities exist within the key issues that surfaced during the internal and external assessments. The strategic planning committee will want to create a matrix that highlights the main themes identified in both assessments. The goal for the committee is to look for relationships, if any, among the themes identified by the internal and external stakeholders. You will want to determine whether common beliefs are shared by both groups or whether themes are clearly divergent. Once these themes have been identified, the committee will need to prioritize the issues, from most to least critical, in terms of the organization's future.

The following terms were presented in Chapter 2:

- **Resources** are human, financial, and capital.
- **Performance** is the evaluation of services or resources provided by the organization.
- **Process** is the strategy or methods used to provide services and resources.

In addition, Chapter 4 provided the four P's:

- **Product** is the resources or services provided by the organization.
- **Place** is the location of services and the system of referrals.
- **Promotion** is the effort needed in formal and informal public relations and fund raising efforts.
- **Price** includes both fees for and costs of providing services or resources.

Internal-External Issue Matrix

The internal-external issue matrix combines both of the previous assessment charts into a format that allows the committee to highlight areas of concern to both assessments. Even if an issue is of concern to only one assessment, that does not make it irrelevant to the strategic planning process. However, the committee should focus initially on the issues that are common to both assessments. This first pass at analyzing the issues might result in a solution that satisfies a broader need than a single-focus issue. The issues that appear on the matrix then need to be prioritized (see Table 6.1).

Translating Issues Into Opportunities

The issues are prioritized based on the perceptions and needs that the strategic planning committee has identified as most crucial for the organization's future. The issues must now be translated into opportunity statements. For example, a product and resource issue statement for a family service agency might be that insufficient resources exist to maintain a very popular teen program. The opportunity statement would then state that expanding the resource base of the teen program would increase the program's capacity to serve those teens who are currently on a waiting list for services.

Table 6.1 Internal-External Issues Matrix

	Resources	**Performance**	**Process**
Product	Product affected by available resources or resources affected by product	Performance affects product value or some product component affects performance	Agency process affects product
Place	Location or referral are affected by available resources	Performance affects the location or availability of services	Agency process affects location or referrals
Promotion	Resources affect formal or informal promotion of agency	Performance affects formal or informal promotion of agency	Agency process affects formal or informal promotion of agency
Price	Resources affects cost of operations	Performance affects cost of operations	Agency process effects cost of operations

Another example for the matrix—addressing process and place is-sues—might be that a well-funded, well-staffed program for adult literacy has few clients who are able to attend classes at the central agency office. The opportunity statement would assert that the delivery of services in the adult literacy program would be greatly enhanced if the program were offered in the outlying rural areas of the community.

Once the key issues have been prioritized, the strategic planning com-mittee will need to compare these opportunities to the organization's current mission statement. If the mission statement and the opportuni-ties are consistent, then the committee will be ready to prepare discus-sion papers on the issues for the upcoming retreat. If the opportunities conflict in some fashion with the mission statement, then the committee will need to evaluate the opportunity and the accompanying need perhaps to revise the mission statement.

Mission statements are the visionary force behind a nonprofit orga-nization, even though the mission may change over time, depending on the organization's and the community's changing needs. The perception of the organizational mission may have altered over time or different stakeholders may place different emphases on various components of the organizational mission. The organizational mission will be addressed in greater detail in Chapter 7, which deals with the pending retreat. At this point in the process, to prepare materials for further discussion, we need the strategic planning committee's best efforts at determining the current mission and the appropriateness of future action based upon this mission.

If the assessments indicate that a new opportunity requires a modification of the existing mission statement, then the committee will need to determine the opportunity's true value. If it is substantial, then the opportunity will need to be prepared for discussion at the retreat. If the opportunity is not critical, then the committee may decide to eliminate it from discussion now and evaluate it at a later time.

Identifying Strategic Target Opportunities

For the purposes of strategic planning, the target opportunities need to be greater in scope and purpose than the resolution of a temporary crisis. The target opportunities should present the organization enough latitude to strategically address an issue that has relevance to the future direction and goals of the agency. A strategic response to an issue or opportunity is one in which the future actions are assessed and deemed desirable for the organization, based on the benefits and costs of both action and inaction.

If we revisit the two opportunities discussed earlier in this chapter, we can frame them as strategic opportunities.

By broadening the resource base of the teen program, the organization would increase the program's capacity to serve teenagers who are currently on a waiting list for services.

In this example, we are highly focused on one program and one waiting list. Although the issues raised may be most appropriate for the teen program, other deserving programs also might benefit from an expanded resource base. The strategic opportunity is to expand the resource base to increase the agency's capacity to offer needed services to members of the target population who are now being underserved. This opportunity will allow the agency room to address the opportunity over the strategic plan's 3- to 5-year time span. The first step may well be addressing the needs of the teen program. Ideally, this will not require many years to complete, and the strategic opportunity will still exist to focus attention on other comparable programs offered by the agency.

Delivery of services in the adult literacy program would be greatly enhanced if the program were offered in the outlying rural areas of the community.

This second example also is highly focused on one service and one location. This organization may wish to address the issue of outreach programs in a larger scope than just the adult literacy program. The strategic opportunity here is to evaluate the feasibility of providing services in outreach settings to serve the unmet needs of clients. This strategic opportunity will allow the organization to reflectively prepare for an expansion of service sites rather than to begin services on a limited basis without preparing for future needs.

Combining the Issues: The Family House

The draft assessments created earlier, along with the financial and market assessments, will be used to create a list of issues facing the organization. In our two samples, the materials presented earlier in the workbook allow you to view easily the key issues raised in the earlier assessments.

Family House Internal Assessment Summary — SUMMARY

The Strategic Planning Committee has completed the Internal Assessment, and the following issues have been raised.

1. *Board of Directors.* Lack of a clear direction for the Board, coupled with the absence of any Board leadership development program, was the greatest concern expressed by Board members. Board members are unclear about the House's future direction.

2. *Staff.* Primary area of concern was the need for resources to increase salary levels and to provide professional development. Staff has many ideas about the House's future but is unclear about how to present these to the Board.

3. *Volunteers.* The agency needs a clear delineation of volunteer and staff roles and greater recognition from the Board regarding the contributions of the volunteers.

4. *Facilities and Equipment.* We have a general need for additional space and equipment to support the House's services; e.g., Board needs a workstation at House; staff needs an additional private area for clinical work and more administrative space.

Family House External Stakeholder Assessment — DRAFT

The interviews and questionnaires have all been completed, and the Strategic Planning Committee has noted the following issues:

1. Our mission is not clearly delineated to the community as a whole. Most frequently the mission was stated as "temporary assistance in domestic violence cases."
2. The increasing incidence of domestic violence in the community has prompted many to wonder why we only serve 15 to 20 families at a time, and why the length of stay is so long.
3. Clients who have been involved with the House for longer than one month speak quite highly of the value of the services. Clients new to the House are more likely to be equivocal in their responses.

Perhaps the most obvious inconsistency between the internal and external assessments concerns the agency's current needs. The internal stakeholders were comfortable with the level of services provided for clients, and yet they felt the need for more space and equipment to meet the house's administrative and service needs. In contrast, the external stakeholders all felt that the house failed to serve the growing need presented by the community. The issue here is differences between internal stakeholders and their comfort level with the current program and external stakeholders who wish for a transition to a shorter in-house program with greater time spent in aftercare.

This issue may be more complex, however, if one considers how these perceptions may have occurred. One critical element is the external stakeholders' perception that the house offers "temporary care", while the internal stakeholders view the program as a major form of clinical intervention. At this point in time, a discussion and consensus about the House's mission might be the most appropriate course of action. Once the House's internal stakeholders are clear about the mission, they can then decide to increase communication with external stakeholders, thereby hoping to change their perceptions. Or they may decide to revisit their program and make changes that are consistent with the interests of the surrounding community.

Although this issue is a critical one, it will require further discussion and review before a plan of action can be determined.

For the strategic planning committee, this issue was framed as an introduction to discussing the House's mission. The committee decided that two primary key issues required further discussion and provided the best target opportunities: (1) the Board's effectiveness and development and (2) resource development and fund raising. Two sample discussion papers have been drafted that provide a starting point for future discussion at the upcoming retreat.

Family House Paper 1

BOARD EFFECTIVENESS AND DEVELOPMENT ISSUES

One of the key findings of the surveys conducted among the Family House Board is the lack of clarity regarding the roles and expectations of its members. In order for the House to function effectively and to best carry out its mission, the Board needs to reach consensus regarding the "job description" that accompanies Board membership.

Corollary findings with respect to Board membership deal with recruiting new members, which is a long-term strategy, and the orientation of new Board members. There was also the expression of need for a complete orientation packet for new Board members so that their participation would be more productive for the House and the committees on which they serve.

Discussion

Policy and organizational tasks have been handled exceedingly well because of the roles of key Board members with extensive experience in handling these matters. However, the Board as a whole expressed a concern about a lack of direction and frequently becomes consumed with the details of agency management rather than seeing the agency from a holistic vantage point. Operational issues have been less consistent and clearly depend on the committee chair's capabilities and commitment. In the past two years, fund raising and special events have been quite successful, primarily because of the committee chair. However, there are no plans in place to train new chairs or Board officers to replace these positions when current terms of office expire.

Resources the Board members need to increase commitment and purpose: (1) a workstation at the House with a computer and phone; (2) a program for developing leadership skills to ease the transition of committee chairs and officers; and (3) an orientation packet for new members that clearly explains the time and expertise required to successfully fulfill Board obligations.

Questions

1. What are the tasks that define the job responsibilities of (a) Board members? (b) committee chairs? (c) executive committee members?

Table 6.2 Family House Internal-External Issues Matrix

	Resources	Performance	Process
Product	• Staff salaries affect recruiting of more male staff and respite care	• Lack of space for clinical services and client dependency issues	• Lack of clarity between staff and volunteer roles in service promotion
Place	• Staff salaries and the ability to expand or modify House setting		
Promotion		• Current performance of program not deemed culturally diverse	• Lack of clarity about House's future inhibits Board support of agency • Lack of clarity in staff and volunteer roles seen by community
Price	• Fees and insurance reimbursements may affect House's future	• Lack of space for Board, agency PR, and fund raising	

2. How can the Family House best develop its Board to successfully lead the House into the next decade?

3. What type of orientation program would be acceptable to Board members and have the greatest likelihood of developing new members' leadership skills?

4. How can Board members be kept informed of the House's daily operations yet remain focused on the agency's long-term policy needs? What vehicles might increase the Board's ability to focus on policy rather than on operational issues?

Family House Paper 2

RESOURCE DEVELOPMENT AND FUND-RAISING STRATEGIES ISSUES

The Family House has done well financially, having retired two of its three mortgage notes and secured funding for its programs. The historical philosophy of fund raising involved conducting one primary fund raising campaign prior to the House's opening, with the assurance that no future funding requests would be initiated.

Special events and programs have been developed on a small yet successful scale. The results of the internal assessment have indicated a need for expanded facilities and equipment. A new fund raising philosophy that is consistent with the ongoing needs of the House needs to be developed by the Board.

Discussion

Essentially, the House has operated well within its budget, and a base of annual donors has been established through a Friends campaign. The House has an outstanding note of approximately $50,000.

State funding may be less secure based on recent state financial problems, and the $75,000 grant may be reduced in the future. The Board needs to begin planning for a vehicle to replace this base source of income.

The original Board members who conducted the initial fund raising for the House are no longer on the Board. Additionally, the economic climate of the surrounding community has significantly altered, and many of the original corporate donors have been bought by other corporations. Not only have their names changed, but also their corporate identities have altered, thus making the original promise to avoid returning for funding seem inappropriate.

Questions

1. What type of fund raising strategy or strategies would best suit the ongoing needs of the House to accomplish its mission?
2. What types of support are required from the community or staff to assist the Board in implementing a new fund raising strategy?
3. What types of new expenditures are timely and appropriate? How can these needs be factored into the overall fund raising strategy?

Combining the Issues: The Community College Foundation

In many respects, the previous work of the Community College Foundation may have seemed somewhat disheartening because both external and internal assessments reveal that the Foundation is not well identified and its work is not considered vital. The consistency of the perceptions, however, does allow for target opportunities that can significantly affect the Foundation's profile and stature.

Community College Foundation: Internal Assessment Summary

The Strategic Planning Committee has completed the Internal Assessment, and the following themes were noted in the course of our work:

1. There was almost complete agreement that the Foundation has not done an adequate job of promoting the Community College to the community.
2. The Foundation Board wishes to be looked on as a major player in the Community College's future development.
3. The Board members believe that there is an enormous but untapped potential within the present Board.

Community College Foundation: External Stakeholder Assessment — DRAFT

We have just completed our interview of the key external stakeholders and the following issues require further discussion:

1. External stakeholders had difficulty differentiating our Foundation from the numerous other support groups on campus.
2. The use of the funds raised by the Foundation was not viewed as critical by a variety of groups whose members do not feel adequately represented on the campus whether as staffmembers, professors, or students.
3. Clearly, there is a leadership vacuum in the minds of the community leaders regarding who best represents the Community College to the community.

Community College Foundation Paper 1

BOARD EFFECTIVENESS AND DEVELOPMENT

One of the key findings of the surveys conducted among the Community College Foundation Board is the lack of clarity regarding the roles and expectations of its members. In order for the Foundation to function effectively and to best carry out its mission, the Board needs to reach consensus regarding the "job description" that accompanies Board membership.

Corollary findings with respect to Board membership deal with new member recruitment, a long-term Board member acquisition strategy for the Board, and new Board member orientation. There is some feeling among the Board that the Community College Foundation should evolve and become more representative of the alumni. Further, there was expression of need for a complete orientation packet for new Board members so that their participation would be more productive for the Community College Foundation.

Another key issue was the creation and maintenance of closer relationships between the Board members and key Community College administrative, alumni, and student leaders. The Board wishes to have a more intimate understanding of the Community College, campus life, and key Community College programs. The Community College staff also desire to have a deeper relationship with the Foundation Board members, and they recognize that the Board members are important players in the future of the campus.

Finally, several Board members suggested that Board participation would be enhanced by (1) regular meetings on campus, (2) increased familiarity among Board members, and (3) better recognition of contributions and service of current and emeritus Board members.

For Discussion and Consideration:

1. What are the tasks that define the "job responsibilities" of a Community College Board Member?
2. How can the Community College Foundation best develop its Board to meet the challenges of the 1990s?
3. How can the Community College Foundation Board best improve its operating format to provide for meaningful participation by all of its members?
4. What are the recommended vehicles that can be developed to enhance Board member understanding of the Community College?

Community College Foundation Paper 2

OTHER COMMUNITY COLLEGE FUND RAISING GROUPS

The Community College President has expressed his desire for the Community College Foundation to take a position of leadership among all of the fund raising organizations supporting the Community College. Both the President and Board strongly believe that a much greater degree of consensus and coordination is needed among these fund raising organizations in order to best serve the Community College, its students, and the general community.

The President supports the Community College Foundation as the leading organization among all of these groups because the mission of the Community College Foundation best addresses the long-term global needs of the Community College and thus places the Foundation in a position of having a broader perspective than the single-focus fund raising organizations, such as those connected to arts, athletics, and numerous "Friends" groups.

Table 6.3 Community College Foundation Internal-External Issues Matrix

	Resources	Performance	Process
Product	• Untapped potential of Board affects work of Foundation	• Inadequate Board promotion of Foundation and Community College results in low-value product	• Lack of Board involvement with Community College has affected product value
Place		• Lack of autonomy affecting performance	• Lack of autonomy affecting process
Promotion		• Similarity to other groups	• Low profile on campus and in community
Price			

The Community College professional staff generally feel that a spirit of cooperation and coordination exists among these programs. However, the level of communication and coordination has not expressed itself at the level of the Boards of Directors or the Volunteer Officers of these organizations. Improving communication between the Community College Foundation and these other fund raising and support groups can only improve the effectiveness of everyone's commitment to the Community College, and this also would allow the Board members to recognize the value of their participation and support.

For the Community College Foundation to take a leadership position among all of these organizations supporting the Community College, it must take into account the need to build consensus without compromising the autonomy these volunteer organizations feel they require in order to fulfill their missions.

For Discussion and Consideration:

1. How can the Community College Foundation best build effective working relationships with these other fund development groups that support the Community College?
2. How can the Community College Foundation best take the lead in joint planning with these groups?

7

Building Consensus for the Mission

Three key elements require attention when charting a nonprofit organization's future: building leadership, setting a clear agenda, and building a consensus of support for both the leadership and agenda. Throughout the strategic planning process, the work of the committee has focused on these three key elements.

At this point in the strategic planning process, significant steps have been taken to address consensus, leadership, and agendas. The composition of the strategic planning committee was vital in recruiting the influential players in your organization and in setting the stage for future leadership and ownership of the plan. Both components are important to the implementation of the completed strategic plan. Without consensus, however, the strategic plan faces the threat of lying dormant, a fate that would render an entire year's effort fruitless and the organization no better off than when it started.

Building consensus really begins with the formation of the strategic planning committee and the board's agreement on the charge given to the committee. Consensus is further enhanced through a full participation in the internal assessment phase of the planning cycle when all key internal players (board members, staff, and volunteers) give input. The culmination of the process to build consensus rests within the board's retreat, where the strategic planning committee receives the mandate to complete its work.

Mission Statement

One of the most difficult problems faced by nonprofit organizations is the creation of a mission statement or the revision of an existing mission statement.

The chances are 50-50 that your organization had a formal mission statement in use and in general circulation before it began its strategic planning process. Oddly enough, many nonprofit organizations operate without carefully defining their mission statements. Over time, these organizations tend to lose focus and effectiveness because the essential function of a mission is to provide a sense of purpose and direction to the organization.

If your organization does not have a current mission statement, or something that passes for a mission statement, you should refer to the articles of incorporation. Therein you should find the original intent of the founders. This intent may not be well stated, but at least it is a beginning. If the original purpose is well stated, perhaps all it needs is a little fine-tuning to turn it into a mission statement.

Elements of a Mission Statement

All nonprofit organizations are created with a mission or fundamental purpose in mind. Over time, that mission may lose its potency as the daily tasks consume everyone's attention. You may also find that the organization is drifting away from its mission as new programs are initiated. The context of the original needs may have changed because of changes in the environment or the marketplace. If any of the above is the case, then it may be time to re-evaluate or change your mission.

The organization's mission is meant to address some specific type of problem or need on a comprehensive basis. The mission should reflect the organization's commitment to the issue being addressed, both in scope and direction. Implicit in the organization's mission is a value statement that implies that the problem being addressed is significant and warrants organizational attention. Everything your organization does should directly relate to the mission. Every program and activity should reflect the organization's commitment to address this central, pressing problem.

Although the mission should be specific, it should also allow for a variety of potential programs that may address the identified need or problem. Most important, the mission should serve as a source of inspiration for those who are involved in the organization. This inspiration is the basis for the commitment of all stakeholders to advance the organization.

In constructing a mission statement, you must understand the problem that is being addressed. The answers to the following questions provide the framework for the mission statement:

1. What is the identified problem or condition? What was the original condition? Did it change over time?
2. Who is affected? What are their characteristics, location, distribution, and relationship to others?
3. What is the significance of the problem? What is its pervasiveness and scope?

Once you have clarified the problem, you are ready to state your organization's mission. Creating or adapting an organizational mission statement involves handling complex and often competing issues. The greater one's knowledge and familiarity of the organization, the more difficult determining the mission that drives the organization may be. This difficulty arises because familiarity with the organization may prompt one to focus on the specific program or method of addressing the problem rather than on a comprehensive view of the problem that may allow for a broader scope and potentially more strategic analysis. As you work with your own mission statement, keep in mind that your task involves a real intellectual struggle. You will need to be an active investigator of your organization's purpose; juggling complexities and making hard choices are an integral part of this exercise.

If the strategic planning committee as a whole is addressing the mission statement, several potential pitfalls may impede the committee's work. As discussions become more involved, the group may find itself distracted by tangential issues. These issues may relate to traditional expectations of the organization or they may involve political issues about the organization's future. The committee has already had to handle a variety of opinions about the organization, some of which have been approving and others dissenting. To keep the committee focused on the task of framing a mission statement, keep in mind that the mission statement should provide a sense of purpose and incorporate a vision of future accomplishment for the organization as a whole.

The mission statement is not just a convenient public relations or fund raising device. The mission statement provides the sense of purpose for the organization. This sense of purpose is highly motivating and allows both staff and volunteers to feel that their involvement with the organization is worthwhile and provides a fundamental service or resource to the community, without which the community as a whole would suffer. At first, this purpose may seem grandiose, but the intent is to motivate and direct on a comprehensive and extensive basis.

Mission statements also contain a vision of future accomplishment that continue to guide the efforts of the nonprofit over time. Coupled with the sense of purpose, this vision provides meaning and direction to the frequently diverse efforts of an organization. Conversely, when a nonprofit organization lacks a functional mission statement, its efforts may seem fragmented and without any sound rationale.

To ensure that the mission statement provides a sense of purpose and incorporates a vision of future accomplishment, the following questions should be addressed:

1. What is the organization's purpose?
2. Why is this purpose important?
3. What will the organization do to fulfill this purpose?
4. How will the organization benefit the community?

Composing or Revising the Mission Statement

Once the elements of the mission statement have been addressed, composing or revising the organization's mission statement becomes somewhat easier. Through the external assessment, you now have an understanding of the community's need for your organization, which also may help frame your thinking. In other words, the mission should tell the world why your organization is here, and it should convey the spirit of the enterprise.

Mission Statement Exercise: Family House

Part 1

1. What is the identified problem or condition that prompted the formation of the organization?

The identified problem is the existence of various forms of abuse (verbal, psychological, and physical) in families that severely limit family members from leading productive lives.

2. Who is affected by this problem or condition?

The victims of abuse include spouses, children, and the elderly. The manifestations of being a victim include withdrawal, depression, suicide, or becoming an abuser. Family life is disrupted or destroyed by unchecked patterns of abuse. The community pays for this unbroken cycle of violence through increased costs to the criminal justice, welfare, and health care systems.

3. What is the significance of the problem or condition?

The significance of the problem rests in the spiraling cycle of unending domestic violence and the associated human and financial costs.

Part 2

1. What is the purpose of the Family House?

The purpose of the Family House is to restore dysfunctional and abusive families to conditions of emotional and physical health wherein nurturing occurs, family functioning is restored, and abuse disappears.

2. Why is this purpose important?

This purpose is important because the incidence of domestic violence and abuse in the community is high and is going unchecked.

3. What will the Family House accomplish?

We believe that the most appropriate intervention is one that preserves the family unit and assists the family in developing positive interaction skills. The most effective treatment approach has been the communal program followed up by an aftercare program and support groups.

4. How will the Family House benefit the community?

Domestic violence is a behavioral disorder that affects the entire family and has ripple effects on the entire community. Not only must the abuser be treated, but also the victim and family. An abusive relationship indicates a family unit out of balance in its relationships. Domestic violence is also a learned behavior passed from one generation to the next. Unless the cycle is broken, this behavior pattern will persist and spread like any other contagious illness.

We will now take the information developed above and translate it into a mission statement for the Family House:

The mission of the Family House is to break the cycle of domestic violence and abusive relationships among affected families in our community through a comprehensive family-centered treatment approach that restores and promotes healthy relationship development.

Mission Statement Exercise: Community College Foundation

Part 1

1. What is the identified problem or condition that prompted the formation of the organization?

The Community College Foundation was originally formed to solicit, invest, and disburse significant donations made to the Community College. The identified need was to assist the Community College in achieving its goal of providing high-quality educational services to the community.

2. Who is affected by this problem or condition?

The beneficiaries of the fund raising activities of the Foundation are the students who receive financial support and enhanced educational opportunities. The community and community's employers also benefit from the skills and contributions that the Community College graduates offer to their growth and prosperity.

3. What is the significance of the problem or condition?

The significance of the need to raise funds for the Community College rests within the fact that tuition, fees, and local tax support do not provide all of the resources necessary to permit the Community College to be a comprehensive provider of high-quality educational services.

Part 2

1. What is the purpose of the Community College Foundation?

The purpose of the Community College Foundation is to provide leadership to the comprehensive fund raising efforts on behalf of the Community College.

2. Why is this purpose important?

This purpose is important because the availability of donated funds is limited and those dollars that can be raised for the Community College must be put to the most effective use.

3. What will the Community College Foundation accomplish?

The Community College Foundation believes that it can become the primary vehicle through which volunteer leadership is channeled to raise significant and meaningful funds to address the high-priority needs of the Community College.

4. How will the Community College Foundation benefit the community?

The Community College Foundation will benefit the community in two ways: (1) by building the capacity and quality of educational services and programs offered by the Community College and (2) by serving as prudent custodians and stewards of gifts and endowments made to the Community College.

Thus, we might complete the mission statement for the Community College Foundation as follows:

The mission of the Community College Foundation is to assist and promote the development of the Community College by serving as the principal agent through which all major gifts are solicited, managed, and disbursed.

Planning the Board Retreat

By now, through the assessment phases and the opportunity identification process, the strategic planning committee should have a fairly good idea of what the organizational agenda will look like. The task now is to give that agenda some definition and allow the board to provide the input that will be used to write the plan. Having some vision of an outcome that will facilitate the board's final adoption of the strategic plan is important. In other words, the board retreat must be carefully planned and organized so that the consensus required for board ownership and implementation of the strategic plan is ensured. The danger in failing to plan the retreat properly is that board members may become confused or divided rather than reach consensus on where and how to proceed.

The feedback received during the internal assessment phase is the best asset for retreat planning. When this feedback is meticulously recorded for each individual board member, you will become aware of the issues, agendas, and biases that will be carried into the event.

Planning for the retreat also will require that you be prepared to keep focused on the central themes of the retreat while you find a way to handle other issues that may be brought up by the participants. These central themes have already been identified through the target opportunities section as well as the mission assessment that was just discussed.

Despite the best planning efforts, discussions can lose focus or tangential issues can suddenly dominate attention. The easiest way to handle these issues without offending participants or diminishing the issue's importance is to record these issues for later discussion. A large pad or writing surface can be made available during the retreat sessions where these other issues can be recorded. In this manner, the issues are not ignored; in fact, they can be referred to by the audience if so desired. The issue has not been ignored, it has only been postponed. The board members will understand that they already have enough material for the full-day retreat that will require their attention. These new issues will be addressed at a later date.

The Board Retreat

Any board retreat used for strategic planning should be a full-day meeting. It should be planned well in advance to facilitate complete attendance by the board. Select a location, such as a hotel or conference center, that has the facilities to handle a group of your board's size comfortably for main sessions, breakout groups, and meals. We recommend that board retreats be planned on weekends. Saturdays are ideal because the distractions of the business day are eliminated and you have the participants' full attention.

The invitation to the retreat should come from the board chair and be presented as the single most important board event of the year, one that requires each member's attendance. The invitation is presented in a personalized letter that identifies the importance of attendance as well as summarizes the decision of the board to engage in the strategic planning process and the significance of the retreat in establishing the organization's future. These letters should be signed by the board chair. Telephone follow-up should confirm RSVPs to ensure complete attendance.

The board retreat is typically organized as shown in Table 7.1.

Materials Needed

Assembling briefing materials is an important part of your preparations for the board retreat. During the course of the strategic planning process before the retreat, the strategic planning committee will have documented the findings of each stage of research and deliberations. These summaries should be included in the retreat materials.

Table 7.1   Typical Board Retreat Schedule

Morning session
- Reception and continental breakfast
- Introductory remarks by board chair
- Goals for retreat explained by executive director
- Presentation by chair of strategic planning committee
- Planning process reviewed
- Key findings of internal and external assessments
- Presentation of key issues for discussion
- Discussion groups led by members of strategic planning committee

Lunch

Afternoon session
- Discussion of group reports and recommendations
- Full board discussion of recommendations
- Summary of key consensus items by board chair
- Wrap-up by chair of strategic planning committee

The uppermost consideration in preparing materials for board study before the retreat is keeping the information package focused on the key issues which board members must resolve and reach agreement.

We recommend that board briefing packets be prepared and mailed approximately 10 days before the retreat. The briefing packets should contain the items shown in Table 7.2, most of which have already been developed in previous chapters.

Each board member should be instructed to review the briefing packet thoroughly before the retreat and to be prepared to participate in an active discussion.

We have found it to be a helpful technique to use topics contained in the briefing papers as tools for small board-discussion groups. When led by members of the strategic planning committee, these smaller groups help to ensure that everyone participates in the day's consensus-building process.

As you plan the retreat, preselect these discussion groups for board members who are likely to have strong interests in one issue rather than another. The discussion leader should also be briefed on the group's composition, the importance of the group process, and the need for and dynamics of getting everyone involved.

Table 7.2 Contents of Retreat Briefing Packets

- Cover letter from board chair stating retreat objectives, its location, and any logistics
- Letter from strategic-planning committee chair summarizing the planning process and introducing key issues for consideration and discussion
- Agenda for retreat
- Mission statement (or proposed revision)
- Briefing papers on key issues (usually 1-page summaries that pose questions for board discussion) (see Chapter 6)
- Copies of any committee reports written during course of the planning process (may include summary reports of board member interviews, internal assessment, and external assessment) (see Chapters 1, 2, 3)
- Any exhibits or appended items such as data tables or charts that might be important to subject matter (see Chapters 1, 2, 3)

Even though small groups allow members to become actively engaged in the discussions, some members may play too dominant a role and thus deny full participation by less vocal members. The discussion leader must monitor the participation levels of all group members and actively solicit input from less vocal members. If one member is intent on taking over the group and a contest of wills occurs between the group leader and a group member, then a few options are available. The vocal member may be asked to record the "Other Issues" discussed earlier; writing down comments interferes with orally controlling a group. The group leader may request assistance from another committee member in keeping the discussion group moving forward. Two committee members may be needed to ensure that the small group process occurs as planned!

Using a Facilitator

Your organization may choose to use the services of a professional facilitator to lead you through the retreat. If you elect to use such an individual, he or she must clearly understand the objectives of the retreat and be well versed in the organization itself. The danger in using facilitators for retreats is that they may take control and lead you to a conclusion that is not consistent with strategic planning committee's desires. A professional and experienced facilitator will work with you before the retreat to assist you in achieving your desired outcomes.

Furthermore, a good facilitator will not steal the show; he or she will play a supportive role to the organization's existing leaders, thus leaving the board a stronger and more cohesive group.

Using the Mission Statement

Perhaps the most fundamental discussion that can be held at a retreat deals with the organization's mission statement. No other question can pose as much debate as "Why are we here?"

The mission statement should be included in the retreat packet only as a draft document. We recommend that some time be set aside toward the end of the day so that the board has a chance to comment on the draft statement after it has discussed other issues.

The strategic planning committee should record all of the comments on the mission statement and incorporate as many of them as possible. Within reason, the actual wording of the statement is not as important as the act of agreeing on the concepts it should espouse. Be wary of permitting a pride of authorship to cloud the real objective of obtaining board ownership of the key issues that will be addressed by the mission statement and the strategic plan. The key here is, first, gathering input that can be edited later to ensure acceptance of the final completed strategic plan and, second, ensuring enough flexibility in the mission statement to allow for the plan's goals and objectives.

Handling the Unexpected

Remember that the board retreat is an event. Like any event, it can be a target for gremlins. All of us can tell horror stories about snafus and incidents that have ruined such affairs. Board retreats also can be spoiled, so your best defense against the unexpected is preparedness.

First, focus on what can happen in the group process. By nature, a retreat is an event designed to elicit participation. The participation you are seeking, however, must stay focused and lead to a positive result. But the focus and outcome you are seeking can be lost if one or more participants engage in disruptive behaviors. How should you handle these behaviors? The following sections deal with disruptive behaviors we have observed and offer suggestions for dealing with them.

Inattentiveness. This problem might be exhibited by someone reading a newspaper during a presentation or by two or more people holding unrelated discussions during the retreat. Mobile or cellular telephones are also threats to a good retreat when they are used to transact personal business during the group process. *Solution:* Engage the offending party directly with a question: "Bob, what do you think about this issue?"

Grenade Throwing. Every now and then, we all encounter someone who views his or her role to be that of "grenade thrower." Usually, this person will wait until the group has just about reached a consensus and then proclaim the entire discussion to be senseless. This is purely and simply a power play. *Solution:* Accept the input graciously and then restate where the group is trying to go or what it is trying to achieve. Ask the grenade thrower to contribute to the positive suggestions that others have made to build a consensus solution. Stroke him or her while reinforcing the group's position: "That's a good thought, Mary. I think Bob was trying to address the same concern when he suggested that we proceed in this direction. How would you suggest that we combine your input with our previous discussion to reach the objective?"

Sidetracking. A group can become sidetracked during a discussion in many ways. Have you ever been in a meeting when someone announced that a close friend has just been diagnosed with cancer? Or perhaps a major sporting event is at hand and everyone wants to talk about it? Or something dramatic has just happened that has captured everyone's attention? Such events can distract from the business at hand if not acknowledged quickly and with a firmness that redirects attention back to the issue at hand. Obviously, some distractions will require heroic efforts to overcome. From personal experience, we have seen well-planned meetings go awry from the influence of political events, during which no one could concentrate from the crush of media representatives pressing for an explanation of some aspect of the organization's functioning. During such instances, the group leader must keep the group focused on the task.

A group discussion can also be sidetracked by an individual who spontaneously addresses unrelated issues. You probably know the type—bubbly and effusive—who will introduce an idea and hold firm to it even though it is not relevant to the discussion. *Solution:* Visibly record the idea on an easel labeled "Other Issues" and then return to the main discussion. These other items can be dealt with later by the board or a board committee.

Withholding and Polarizing. Group discussions can be less than effective in achieving consensus if you encounter withholders or polarizers.

Withholders generally can be spotted by their crossed arms, scowling faces, and closed mouths. A second type of withholder is simply a wallflower and is too intimidated to participate. Both types must be personally drawn out by the discussion leaders.

Polarizers can be spotted by the extreme positions they take in discussions. Polarizers are dangerous because they can effectively table a discussion by taking an absolutist position that is intolerable to the group, whose members cannot persuade the polarizer to moderate his or her stance. The net result is a standoff. *Solution:* Remind everyone of the goal of producing a consensus position: "In 15 minutes, we must give the main group our recommendation, so let's concentrate on a compromise."

The best way to prepare for the unexpected is to have more than one individual responsible for keeping things on track. This task usually is delegated to agency staff. If you have not had much experience in putting on events, ask for assistance from someone who plans and arranges events regularly. Chances are that this individual has seen it all and can work effectively to prevent mishaps before they occur or can respond quickly when the lights go out.

8

Setting Goals and Objectives

Before we address goals and objectives, let us review what has been accomplished to date in the strategic planning process. The internal and external assessments have provided a wide array of information and issues that address the organization from every conceivable vantage point. All of the stakeholders and constituencies have had a role in assessing the organization, both in its present capacity and with an eye toward its future needs.

These assessments were compared and contrasted, and the ensuing issues were identified. The issues were framed first as target opportunities and then as strategic opportunities. The strategic opportunities were then compared to the existing mission statement, and any modifications were proposed and analyzed. Discussion papers were created and presented at the board retreat, where further discussion groups were formed and the opportunities were given careful and deliberate attention. The results of the retreat were:

- consensus on the organization's essential purpose and guiding vision (its mission statement)
- consensus on strategic opportunities
- renewed vigor and enthusiasm by board members on their roles in the organization and its future
- consensus for action—that is, for completing the strategic planning process.

At this point, the task facing the strategic planning committee is to translate this consensus for action into logical and concrete steps that will allow the action to take place. In and of itself, identifying a strategic opportunity does not provide a clear, thoughtful methodology to address the opportunity.

Overview of Goals and Objectives

To accomplish anything, you need a clear vision of the desired outcome. Goals represent ideals, which are the organizational commitment to a desired future state or condition. To use an analogy, goals represent the organization's desired destination and the objectives are the strategic steps required to reach the destination. To travel from the "here and now" and arrive at the "there and future" requires that your organization plot a travel plan that best addresses the identified issues and opportunities. The specific route your organization takes depends on the tasks that you wish to accomplish along the way. A variety of travel routes may allow you to ultimately arrive at your destination. The points along the routes are the necessary objectives to be accomplished for the organization to reach its goals and final destination (see Figure 8.1).

The time frame for the strategic planning process typically is 3 to 5 years. Therefore, the goals must reflect this time frame and allow for continued efforts on the part of the organization over this period. The goals should address opportunities that will allow the organization to position itself in the future.

The objectives also provide the specific methodology or strategy that will be implemented to arrive at each goal. The objectives are sequential and provide the milestones that will permit the organization to determine if the process is on track or if it has derailed at some point.

Translating the Retreat's Outcomes Into Goals

The board retreat produced a list of opportunities that the board deemed worthy of addressing. The work of the strategic planning committee is to translate these opportunities into goals that will guide the organization over the next 3 to 5 years.

Despite the number of opportunities that may have been identified during the retreat, a small to medium-sized nonprofit organization may

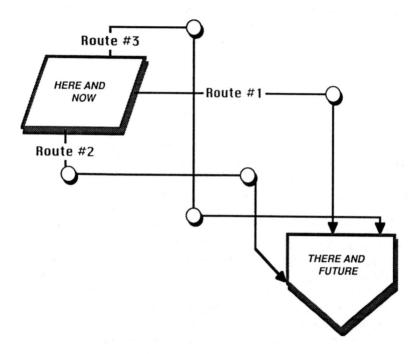

Figure 8.1. Routes From Here to There

only be realistically able to identify three goals that will be addressed over the next 5-year period. Please remember that these goals will be implemented by a variety of different objectives. The organization will have many tasks to address over the next 3 years.

How will the committee translate the results of the board retreat into strategic goals? One way to approach this question is to mentally leap into the future and imagine that 3 years have passed and that your organization is successful and thriving. Three years from now, what major accomplishments can you look back on with pride? Quantify these accomplishments and identify why they are important. You could answer this question using broad themes or the committee could compose a brief narrative that envisions your organization's accomplishments and work 3 years from now. This vision should incorporate the predominant opportunities and desires raised during the course of the retreat.

For example, if you expanded your facility, one accomplishment might be that 25% more clients received services that allowed them to obtain employment and be self-supporting. If you trained your board in fund raising skills, then you might be able to note that $300,000 was raised, a sum that allowed your organization to provide 2 years of meals to home-bound elderly clients. If you expanded your staff, you might be able to claim that 45 additional children left your waiting list and received day care services.

The outcome of this "visioning" exercise will provide you with a perspective of your successful agency. Now return to this vision and highlight the three phrases or concepts that most clearly describe the agency's successes and accomplishments.

This list represents your organization's goals—that is, its guides for the direction it will take over the next 3 years. At some future point, you may adapt or alter these goals, but for now they are your best intentions for the organization. Your next step will be charting a course that allows you to accomplish these goals.

Visioning Exercise: Family House

Three years from now, what has the Family House accomplished and why are these accomplishments important?

The Family House has continued to provide intensive clinical services and aftercare to abusive families. Our program is highly innovative and successful. The House operates at 90% of capacity. The program is well regarded by the community and all referral groups; there is a complete understanding of our program and the methods used to provide services. Our board has been particularly helpful in communicating our program to external stakeholders, as well as leading the House toward continued development of high-quality programming, recruitment of culturally diverse staff, creation of successful resource-development activities, and guidance for the volunteer program.

The board has instituted a resource-development program and endowment fund with combined assets of $750,000. Our staff is committed; turnover is low and salaries, facilities, and benefits have combined with the high-quality program to make employment with the House highly desirable. The volunteer program is valued in the community, and we have an active recruitment program. These accomplishments are important because they plan for a secure future for the

House with respect to community support, referrals, client satisfaction, and staff and volunteer recruitment and retention.

Using the paragraphs above, identify three themes or concepts that indicate desired states for the future.

1. The Board leads the House and guides efforts for program development, fund raising, public relations, and volunteer and staff recruitment.

2. Staff salaries, benefits, House facilities, and the successful program combine to make employment desirable.

3. Program is highly regarded and continues successful intervention strategies for abusive families.

Convert these themes into goals for the Family House.

1. Create and develop a board leadership and development program that will provide the Family House with exceptional guidance, support, and resources.

2. Enhance and develop an extraordinary staff program to ensure the highest quality of program and service delivery for clients.

3. Create methods to share the successful House program on a regional and national basis and create vehicles for encouraging further House program development.

Visioning Exercise: Community College Foundation

Three years from now, what has the Community College Foundation accomplished and why are these accomplishments important?

The Community College Foundation is clearly identified as the leading support organization representing the Community College. The Foundation has conducted campus programs designed to develop future plans for the Community College and has developed the volunteer resources necessary to make those plans a reality. Three focus groups were held, and the results were translated into action steps by the Board.

The Foundation has just completed a highly successful capital campaign that has mobilized community support and greatly enhanced the quality of educational services offered on campus. The capital campaign raised $1 million in resources and pledges. The work of the Foundation is highly regarded and valued by both internal and external stakeholders. Requests for Board membership have increased, and the Board is now perceived as active and capable, with the leadership and skills required to provide dynamic support for the Community College.

The importance of these accomplishments can be viewed within the context of the needs of the community for quality education and the needs of the Community College for resources and support necessary to provide quality educational services.

Using the above responses, identify three themes or concepts that indicate desired states for the future.

1. Foundation board is active, capable, and the leading representative of the Community College.

2. Foundation has a successful capital campaign.

3. Foundation and resources are valued by campus and community.

Convert these themes into goals for the Community College Foundation.

1. Develop and conduct successful capital campaign for the Community College.

2. Create and develop a Board development program that informs, motivates, and compels Board members to act as leaders on behalf of the Community College.

3. Provide resources based on the identified needs of the campus and the community.

Creating Objectives to Accomplish Goals: Mapping a Route

Now that you have articulated your organization's goals, a plan of action is required to move toward these desired outcomes. This plan of action is composed of supporting objectives and action agendas that define what must be done, when it must be done, who is responsible for doing it, and who will verify the completion of the tasks. Together these elements compose the "strategy" in the strategic plan. They answer the question of how the organization gets from "here and now" to "there and future."

Objectives are specific measurable statements of accomplishments within a given time frame. They are tools for measuring your progress.

An objective has the following characteristics:

1. It quantifies a condition and indicates how that condition will be reduced, increased, or altered.

2. It describes an achievable state that can be reached through change.

3. It does not provide a service, but it does change a condition.
4. It operationalizes a goal.
5. It uses numbers or percentages when referring to change.

In much the same way, a traveler planning a trip from New York to Los Angeles must organize a series of events that will occur in sequence so that he or she can reach the destination. This sequence of events (objectives) might be as follows:

1. Call the airline and order tickets
2. Pay for tickets
3. Book hotel reservations in Los Angeles
4. Arrange for someone to receive mail and feed pets while I'm gone
5. Pack suitcase
6. Call for taxi to airport
7. Go to airport
8. Check in for flight
9. Board aircraft
10. Arrive in Los Angeles
11. Take taxi to hotel
12. Check into hotel

Steps 1 through 12 above represent one strategy for achieving the goal of arriving in Los Angeles. Note, however, that the strategy could be altered by selecting train travel, choosing to fly nonstop as opposed to making connections, or driving oneself to the airport. The point is that many options or routes run toward the ultimate goal. Preparing objectives (setting a strategy) for achieving your organization's goals is much the same.

Selecting the best strategy (set of objectives) to reach your goal requires that you apply the following parameters to the process of logical reasoning:

What are the resource limits, if any, that affect the strategy?
What obstacles may affect the strategy?
Does the strategy capitalize on the organization's strengths?

Let us now apply the technique to one of the goal statements for the Family House. Note that the objectives are presented in a chronological sequence that indicates the path the organization will follow to reach the goal. For additional examples, see the completed strategic plans in the Appendix.

Family House Goal Statement

Create and develop a board leadership and development program designed to provide the Family House with exceptional guidance, support, and resources.

GOAL STATEMENT OBJECTIVES:

1. Conduct survey of similar organizations nationally to gather information on board leadership and development programs by January 199x. *Responsibility:* Executive Director.
2. Prepare report on survey findings by February 199x. *Responsibility:* Executive Director.
3. Appoint ad hoc Board Leadership and Development Committee by March 199x. *Responsibility:* Board Chair.
4. Hire consultant to assist the ad hoc Committee in designing a Board Leadership and Development Program by April 199x. *Responsibility:* ad hoc Committee Chair.
5. Present consultant and Committee recommendations to the Board for approval by August 199x. *Responsibility:* ad hoc Committee Chair.
6. Implement recommendations as approved by the Board beginning September 199x. *Responsibility:* Executive Director.

In devising this strategy, we considered the need to help the board along in its quest for a higher level of effectiveness by placing the impetus to begin the process in the hands of the executive director. The strategy also calls for the involvement of a consultant to help the board crystallize a workable program. Finally, we placed the go-ahead decision firmly with the board while giving responsibility for final implementation to the executive director, thus helping to ensure follow through on the implementation decision.

Establishing Responsibility for Implementing Objectives

Although the board retreat provided the forum for developing the organizational goals, the resulting objectives will be implemented by various board committees. These committees may need additional structure or support to ensure that they are successful in formulating the objectives that are needed to reach the desired goals. Most organizations have a committee structure of board members, staff, and volunteers who are responsible for accomplishing specific tasks for the organization. Although a committee may request that all internal stakeholders assist in some manner with an activity, the committee itself is responsible for organizing the efforts and coordinating activities that are contained in a specific objective.

Depending on your organization's sophistication and needs, you may or may not have a highly developed board committee structure. How many committees should a board have? Only as many as are needed to accomplish the board's objectives! This will also depend on the size of your board and how willing you are to recruit outside volunteers to serve on committees. One way for the board to recruit new members is to first have them serve on a committee as community volunteers. This method is also very helpful for determining whether prospective board members truly have an interest in serving on a board.

Table 8.1 shows the basic types of committees that function in a nonprofit organization.

Determining which committee should have responsibility for specific tasks is not always easy. For example, the Speakers Bureau uses volunteers, raises money, and increases public awareness of the organization. The committee that is ultimately responsible for overseeing the Speakers Bureau also must coordinate activities with several other committees to ensure that everyone is aware of specific activities or accomplishments.

Recognizing donor or volunteer accomplishments may be the task of the fund raising committee, the volunteer committee, or the public relations committee. An essential step is to have the executive committee outline which committee will handle which tasks and how coordination of efforts will occur. These decisions can then be altered over time if changes warrant.

If the executive committee has not determined committee responsibilities, it will fall to the strategic planning committee to develop these responsibilities in conjunction with the strategic plan. The strategic planning committee should attempt to respond to this task with a view toward building organizational structure rather than responding to the current committee chairs and individual members of specific committees. The temptation always exists to use particularly productive board members for important organizational tasks. However, a potential problem may arise: Is a personality issue masking as an organizational issue?

Table 8.1 Basic Types of Committees in Nonprofit Organization

Executive committee
Generally composed of officers and several at-large members (or committee chairs); this committee is responsible for overseeing other committees and coordinating all actions of board.

Finance committee
Composed of treasurer and several others who oversee financial needs of organization; this committee prepares annual report, handles annual audit, and is responsible for corporate investments and cash flow.

Public relations committee
This committee actively seeks to generate community awareness of organization: its mission, programs, and services provided to the community.

Fund raising committee
This committee organizes, conducts, and evaluates all fund raising ventures sponsored by the organization and may coordinate efforts of community groups raising funds on organization's behalf.

Nominating committee
This committee searches for new board members in community, provides the board with information about suitable candidates, and nominates board officers for annual elections.

Volunteer committee
This committee coordinates volunteer schedules and recognizes achievements by individual volunteers.

Planning committee
This committee incorporates the planning process as a regular organizational function.

Operations committee
This committee oversees needs of buildings and facilities as well as sets policy for service delivery and staff.

This strategic planning process is designed to provide a completed plan before annual plans are developed or committee chairs or board officers are nominated. The strategic plan thus has the capability of addressing organizational needs and providing for the restructuring of responsibilities. Once the plan has been accepted, the nominating and annual planning process can reflect the desired organizational changes rather than the existing personalities of current board members in leadership positions.

9

Completing the Strategic Plan

Drafting the Strategic Plan

In the previous chapters, you assessed your organization's strengths and weaknesses, highlighted potential opportunities, examined your mission statement, and drafted goals and objectives. You are now ready to assemble a working document that will allow others to have final input in your organizational agenda. In essence, you are preparing to transfer ownership of this plan from the strategic planning committee to all of the organization's internal and external stakeholders.

The document you are about to prepare has all but written itself as the result of the steps you have previously completed in the strategic planning process. Thus, what remains to be completed should be viewed more in terms of "packaging" the results of the process rather than creating anything new.

The format for the draft strategic plan differs sequentially from the planning process presented by this workbook, because the planning process itself needs to provide your organization with a structure that will allow the greatest flexibility while addressing both internal and external issues for the organization. The written strategic plan, however, needs to be easily read and understood. The discussions and issues need to be framed within a report so that the reader can easily understand the information presented. The following items provide a format for you to adapt your results from the previous exercises and prepare a working draft document.

Executive Summary

Create a brief summary of the purpose of the document and outline the desired outcome. You may also wish to summarize the efforts and process that led to the strategic plan document that acknowledges the participation and influence of the board and other key groups.

Mission Statement

Insert the mission statement that has been drafted or modified as a result of the board retreat. In a brief yet compelling manner, elaborate on your organization's mission and provide the reader with a concrete vision of your organizational purpose. A historical note also may be desirable that details the reasons, need, or problem that prompted the community to create your organization.

External Assessment

The exercises completed as part of the external assessment need to be combined into a narrative that discusses the environment in which your organization functions. Discuss how the organization receives clients, who generates referrals, and what types of competing or complementary services exist in the community. Describe any regulatory or legal factors that have a bearing on your organization's present or future operations. Try to create an accurate picture of the environment as it presently interacts with and affects your organization. This step requires little more than updating the external assessment summary previously written and distributed as part of the briefing materials for the board retreat.

Internal Assessment

The exercises completed in the internal assessment should be integrated in a discussion of your organization's operation. Typically, you would highlight the topics shown in Table 9.1 and, after each one, add the strategic opportunities for growth or change identified by your board and strategic planning committee.

Table 9.1 Highlighted Internal Assessment Topics

Types of services offered
Who uses these services and any unique features about either clients or services.

Organizational staffing
Services provided by staff and their unique qualifications and roles within organization.

Volunteer roles
With clients, community members, and funding or regulatory sources.

Board of directors
Responsibilities, organization, leadership, training, and recruitment.

Facilities and equipment
Describe general state of facilities and equipment and ability to offer services or resources.

Operating procedures and policies
Discuss any new policies or needed changes in organizational structure.

Financial overview
Include information gathered during previous phases that assists reader in understanding organization's current status and future needs.

Fund raising programs
Discuss past, present, and future fund raising efforts and plans.

Goals

Here you would insert the goal statements that you completed in Chapter 8.

Strategic Objectives

Now add the objectives supporting the goals as you developed them in the previous chapter. Remember to present the objectives for each goal sequentially and include who will be responsible for accomplishing the objective and what time frame has been set for its completion.

Conclusion

Discuss the plan's overall impact on your organization, the client community, and the general community. This is an appropriate place to insert the language you created as part of the visioning exercise in Chapter 6. This conclusion to the strategic plan reiterates your concrete vision of future success.

Appendices

Add any tables or charts that are relevant to the strategic plan. Keep in mind that your readers will constitute a broad audience with varying levels of interest and knowledge of your organization. The charts and tables should be easily understood and related to issues raised in the strategic planning process regarding past, present, and future performance.

Gaining Final Acceptance

Now the strategic planning committee is ready to discuss this draft strategic plan with the various constituencies and stakeholders who have interests in your organization.

Why do you need additional constituent support at this point? You may feel that you have already accurately incorporated the issues raised in the internal and external assessments and are now ready to approve the draft plan and begin implementation. In fact, if the strategic planning committee has treated everyone's input conscientiously and has successfully engendered consensus throughout the process, then the draft plan almost certainly will enjoy broad-based support. Ideally, board members should feel as if the completed strategic plan is feeding back to them the messages and themes that arose from the process to build a consensus for moving the organization forward.

The reality, however, is that you need to "test the waters" and make a final determination about any opposition that may exist and what form that opposition may take. Consensus building involves organizational politics, and political issues can shift and emerge with great speed in any nonprofit organization. In addition, changes in the environment may warrant attention in your completed strategic plan.

The working draft of the strategic planning document should be presented to a variety of people, and their interests and commitment levels to the ideas should be evaluated. Specifically, the questions presented in Table 9.2 should be probed with the stakeholders after they read the draft strategic plan.

Frequently, the best ideas can fade away under opposition to a tangential issue. For example, the draft plan may contain a wonderful

Table 9.2 Questions for Stakeholders

- Will donors support ideas contained within plan? What level of support can be anticipated?
- Will staff support program issues contained within plan?
- Do board members, committee chairs, and volunteers feel they have clearly defined roles within the strategic plan that provide goals, objectives, and motivation for further organizational involvement?
- Do members of client communities feel that plan addresses their needs and allows for continued involvement with services or resources provided by organization?
- Do referral or regulatory entities feel plan responds to their organizational needs, thus allowing them to work in complementary fashion with your organization?
- Does plan spark enthusiasm and interest in community leaders and members who do not presently have active roles in organization? If so, how might they see themselves as becoming involved with organization?

---

fund raising idea, but when it is presented to the board or donors it fails to receive a favorable response because of other "hidden" issues contained within the plan. These hidden issues may have nothing to do with fund raising and yet they may prevent stakeholders from adopting or supporting the completed strategic plan.

If some board members feel that they want to change the character of the board in some fashion, then they may resist attempts to start working on new ideas until they accomplish their own goals. The strategic planning committee needs to know these issues before the draft strategic plan is presented for final board approval. The committee may need to respond by either incorporating the other issues or addressing them directly. Remember that your ultimate goal is to create a workable, achievable plan for organizational development. The work of the past six months should not be abandoned because of changing political issues within the organization or within the community.

The strategic planning committee may need to incorporate new suggestions into the final document as a result of the responses to the draft. In the event that someone uncovers hidden agendas and barriers to acceptance or implementation, several options are available. If the hidden agendas cannot be addressed at this time, a section can be added in the final plan for areas of future need. For example, if the board wishes to change its size or character over the next several years, this need can be addressed in the final plan as a future need. If the need is one that will solve itself over time (that is, as board terms expire, new members can be appointed), then the organization can handle the concerns without immediately assigning priority to the issue. By identifying the need, the plan allows others to have a voice and a role in the process rather than allowing the hidden agenda to overtake the strategic planning process.

Once the document has been updated, the final version is ready to be presented to the board for approval. The final plan should be mailed out to the board before the meeting in which the plan will be presented for adoption. Presentation of the final strategic plan to the board and the motion for board approval should be made by the chair of the strategic planning committee.

See the Appendix for completed strategic plans for the two sample organizations.

10

Implementing the Plan

Using the Plan: An Overview

How can the final strategic plan be used within your organization? It is a clear statement of your organization's vision for the next several years. The plan has a variety of potential uses for your organization. The plan can be used to recruit new board members to your organization. The plan will provide a clear picture of your organization and allow prospective members to determine ways in which they can best assist your efforts.

The plan can be used as an informational piece for prospective or repeat donors. The plan provides donors with a strategy for organizational development: Major donors can begin to evaluate how they can participate in your organization's overall plan. The plan can serve as a vehicle for discussion with donors, determining what areas spark their interest and thus qualifying donors before the plan is implemented.

The plan can be used as a public relations tool, providing community leaders with information about your service delivery and the needs of clients.

The plan can be used to establish guidelines for individual staff performance, providing a rationale for the performance of key tasks with respect to the organization's overall performance.

The plan provides clients with a blueprint for future services.

The plan provides a clear framework for accomplishment and organizational priorities. In some organizations, new ideas are generated at such a rapid rate that few are ever developed and actually implemented. The plan will focus efforts and minimize random actions.

The plan provides a cohesive vision that will spark the energy and commitment of everyone connected with your organization. Because everyone is represented in some fashion within the plan, they all have an interest in generating the support and enthusiasm required to successfully implement the plan.

Annual Planning

Most nonprofit organizations engage in some level of annual planning, whether it be as simple as formulating a budget or as sophisticated as producing a lengthy document filled with goals, objectives, and action agendas.

Properly implemented, the strategic plan is the framework within which annual planning and budgeting occur. The progress of the organization toward meeting the plan's goals and objectives is the departure point from the strategic planning process to the annual planning or budgeting process.

Quite simply, annual operating plans and annual budgets must address those incremental steps that your organization will implement during the next 12-month period to move itself toward the strategic plan's long-range goals.

Therefore, the litmus test for an effective annual plan or annual budget is not the format or degree of sophistication, but the level of congruence with the strategic plan.

When examining the draft annual plan or operating budget, look for linkages to the strategic plan and reference those linkages so that everyone in the organization can appreciate the role they play in moving the organization toward a common purpose and clearly identified direction.

At the board level, each committee should establish its own "miniplan" that will outline its activities over the course of the year. This may be the most difficult task of the whole process! Committees need to establish calendars for meeting dates, assign sequential tasks, and monitor their results quite actively. The board president or executive director may wish to create a year-long calendar for all committee meetings early in the year. If committees wait too long, they will be unable to accomplish

Table 10.1 Annual Planning Procedure

Month Activity

Month	Activity
12	Write analysis of event for future consideration
11	Recognize donors and volunteers
10	Hold event
9	Secure all needed donated items and supplies
8	Send out invitations and conduct publicity for event
7	Invitation sent to printers, mailing labels completed
6	Secure site and date; approach event sponsors
5	Create schedule for event; outline volunteer tasks
4	Create event budget
3	Decide on type of event; establish fund raising goal
2	Create an event subcommittee; determine what approval or support is needed from other board committees or staff

their objectives. The board president or executive director can assist this process by meeting with committee chairs, establishing how often each committee will meet, and scheduling the meetings so that they are not in conflict with each other. Many committees will need staff and other board members to periodically join them, so meeting dates need to be scheduled accordingly.

The first committee meeting of the year should focus on annual planning. The committee may need to work backward to schedule the tasks accordingly. For example, suppose the fund raising committee will sponsor a special event in the fall. Scheduling backward from the event would work in the fashion shown in Table 10.1. As you can see, the initial activities that will guarantee the event's success must take place in the second meeting of the year—immediately following the planning meeting! The committee will need to make regular reports as to its progress for the board, both to secure needed assistance and assure everyone that the event really will occur.

You may wish to establish an event subcommittee because the fund raising committee may have other tasks to accomplish in addition to the special event. The fund raising committee may also need to manage the annual membership campaign as well as secure funding through grants or special gifts. All of these tasks are important and require scheduling and coordination to ensure their success.

How are the committee activities monitored? If the committee has a calendar similar to the one above, then the board president or executive director will easily be able to determine if the committee is running smoothly and on schedule. Your organization may wish to have committees report to the board periodically or it may desire to have committee chairs regularly report to the executive committee.

Committees also can generate minutes of their meetings that can be mailed out in regular board packets, summarizing their progress and identifying concerns or problems. Meeting minutes can be very helpful in preparing a future committee for the tasks ahead, providing clear guidance as to previous pitfalls and successes.

If a chair feels that the committee is falling behind or if board members or staff become aware of problems, then try to address these problems directly. The longer the organization waits to solve a problem, the less likely that the strategic plan will be successful.

11

Using the Strategic Plan to Evaluate Organizational Progress and Performance

Evaluating Organizational Progress

The effectiveness of any strategic plan is linked directly with how fully the nonprofit organization accepts it as a dynamic rather than a static instrument. The traits that lend credibility to the strategic plan over time are its validity and usefulness. Furthermore, the strategic plan should be viewed not as an instrument of decision making, but as one that aids the process of decision making. No plan can substitute for good judgment and creativity.

At the end of each year, the organization must evaluate the progress that has been made toward the goals specified in the strategic plan. The strategic plan represents your organization's best efforts at identifying areas that need improvement and development. Yet unforeseen occurrences can affect even the best of plans. Rather than assuming that everything the organization did was somehow ineffective, it needs to closely evaluate its actions to determine whether it still wishes to proceed in the same direction or if a change in course is required.

The first step in this annual evaluation process is to see if the organization achieved, exceeded, or failed to meet its objectives. If the organization either exceeded or failed to meet its expectations, then some adjustments may be needed in the overall strategic plan. This may be particularly true if the cause of the variance from expectations relates to some environmental factor, such as a new or previously unrecognized opportunity or threat. The cause for either exceeding or underperforming against expectations may also be operational in character; if so, some organizational changes are warranted that may or may not affect the strategic plan.

Essentially, the organization must ask itself annually to assess what, if anything, is materially different about the internal and external environments and how such a difference might invalidate the assumptions prevailing when the strategic plan was written. If either environment has changed materially, then the organization is obligated to update the strategic plan. The process of updating the strategic plan need not be as comprehensive as drafting the original document. The exercise can be best handled by the executive committee addressing specific issues.

Some organizations engage in an annual process to update the strategic plan by simply focusing one year ahead. These are generally referred to as "rolling" 3- or 5-year plans.

In the organization's annual evaluation of the strategic plan, market conditions, regulatory conditions, or operating conditions might have changed so dramatically that the original plan simply is no longer valid. In this event, an entirely new plan is called for and the entire strategic planning process should be repeated. Chances are, however, that you will not wait until the end of the year should there be such a drastic change in any of these conditions.

Once again, the need to gather consensus about the success of the strategic plan is a crucial component of any changes or revisions. By returning to the individuals who provided input originally and asking them once again to respond to a series of questions about the development of the organization, the consensus that was developed initially can be reinforced and maintained.

After receiving the responses from relevant constituencies, the organization will need to create a report that evaluates the plan's success. After being shared with the board, the report can be appended to the original plan. Such an appendix updates readers regarding the plan's success. If the plan is rewritten or substantially modified, the introduction should explain why the changes were made.

Sharing Organizational Success

Before your organization begins the next planning or evaluation cycle, publicize your success! If you have a newsletter, share your success with your readers. If you mailed your plan to donors or foundations, send them a letter highlighting your accomplishments. Your organization put a great deal of effort into realizing the goals you outlined: Do not forget to congratulate yourselves on a job well done.

Appendix A

Family House Strategic Plan

1 EXECUTIVE SUMMARY

This strategic plan is a key step toward defining the Family House's future. The purpose of this plan is to set a direction and to delineate the tasks that will help the House achieve its goals.

The Strategic Planning Committee synthesized the interviews, responses, and suggestions of a wide scope of individuals, both within our House and the community, about the House's past, present, and future. This plan details these responses, and its goals and objectives reflect the broad consensus that was reached. The House's mission has been revised to more adequately focus its purpose and direction. One major issue raised within this planning process is the length of the in-house intensive clinical services. Referral and community organizations and leaders feel a shorter in-house program with greater emphasis on aftercare would allow more families to enter the House's program. This key issue will be addressed throughout the first year of this plan.

2 THE FAMILY HOUSE MISSION

The mission of the Family House is to break the cycle of violence and abusive relationships among affected families through a comprehensive family-centered treatment approach that restores and promotes healthy relationships.

The Family House's mission reflects our commitment to family preservation in a safe environment and our belief that families in abusive situations require extraordinary measures. This commitment to families is based on our experience, which indicates that families are most likely to succeed with intensive intervention programs. In addition, we are strongly committed to the concept that families that are allowed to remain intact during intensive intervention have a greater likelihood of remaining so.

3 MARKET ASSESSMENT

The Family House is a unique facility in our metropolitan community as well as in the state. The House serves families exhibiting abusive behaviors. In most cases, these families have been referred to treatment or intervention at least two times before they enter the Family House program. These families enter with specific needs for shelter and intensive clinical intervention, including training, counseling, case management, aftercare, and supervision. In addition, family members benefit from the emotional support available in formal and informal settings from other families in similar situations.

In terms of the overwhelming need for adequate and comprehensive intervention services, the following statistics represent the current situation in Johns County. Last year, 5,000 women and children were turned away from domestic violence shelters because of lack of space. This was double the number of individuals served throughout the county last year. Also last year, police departments reported a 62% increase in arrests because of family violence. Reports of child abuse have tripled in the last year, and the state incidence remains 30% above the national average. Sexual abuse currently affects 1 in 6 children in our community, but 20% of abuse reports are not investigated because of a lack of state funding and staff for services. Abuse of the elderly, especially those living in extended families, also has increased dramatically. At present, the growth of the elderly population in our community is the fourth highest nationally and is more than twice the national average.

Several other facilities also offer shelter for domestic violence victims, but they are unable to adequately address the community's needs. For the elderly and children, state facilities and foster care are available, yet no other program exists that targets the entire family and focuses on keeping the family intact. The state has a model program that provides intensive services in the family home, yet the scope is highly limited to families with no previous history of abuse. Local family service agencies provide counseling and operate an abuse hotline for parents, but no other agency offers the same scope of services as does the Family House.

Overlapping services that do exist in the community are offered by a wide array of agencies and include counseling, substance abuse programs, parent training, and psychiatric counseling. The state protective services provide foster care and some monitoring of families after treatment, although at minimal levels.

Referrals are received from a variety of sources, including local hospitals and attending physicians, court-ordered treatment programs, police departments, the state social service department, agencies offering counseling or parent training, churches and religious organizations, and domestic violence shelters. As mentioned earlier, all of these entities provide services that address one component of the overall problem that affects families caught in abusive patterns.

The Family House is unique because we offer services to the entire family in our facility. Families reside at the House together, although victims and abusers are initially separated within the House. The family is reunited once the staff and the family members feel that they can safely live together. Our professional staffing is far more intensive than other agencies serving the same population. Our uniqueness is our focus on clinical services for the entire family, maintaining the family in one setting throughout treatment, and providing a thorough aftercare program.

The Family House has a 90% success rate: The families remain intact, and abusive behaviors are eliminated.

4 OPERATIONAL ASSESSMENT

4.1 Service Analysis

The Family House provides services to families in abusive situations. Sadly, we have no "typical" client. For spousal abuse, parents generally have only a high school education, although 25% have some higher education. Generally, the mother is a homemaker, and the family income level ranges from lower- to upper-middle class, depending on the father's earning level. Marriages are generally 10 to 15 years in duration, and there are 2 to 3 children per family.

Child abuse shows no clear trends, but most victims (75%) are girls, and the abuser is primarily either a family member or a boyfriend living in the home. For elderly abuse, most families are middle class but lack the financial resources to place elderly relatives in a supervised living arrangement. Most of our clients

(80%) have been referred to treatment at least twice before they enter the Family House program.

The vast majority of the adults involved come from abusive homes and are repeating a pattern of abuse. Families come to the House seeking control and relief from their abusive and often escalating problems. Families who enter our program are generally quite compliant with treatment, especially because their only other option may be court-ordered separation. Families remain in the House for 6 to 8 weeks of intensive care followed by aftercare in their homes, with continued monitoring for 8 months after completion of the program.

The unique features of our program are that families remain intact throughout the treatment and aftercare follow-up. The recidivism rate is exceedingly low: 90% of families completing the entire program have remained abuse-free 18 months after completing the program. Approximately 10% of all families accepted into the House fail to complete the entire program. Once a family fails to comply with the program, it is not eligible for return. The waiting list and need for services are too great to allow repeated attempts at intervention for families who lack the motivation to comply with the program's objectives.

While families are living in the House, they are encouraged to maintain all aspects of their independent living obligations. Families cook their own meals at the House and are responsible for housekeeping details in their living quarters.

4.2 Staffing

The Family House has 10 full-time employees: an executive director, a day manager, a night manager, two clinical supervisors, and five social workers or counselors who provide direct services to families. Social workers are assigned to specific families and provide the aftercare services to the assigned family once it leaves the House. The two clinical managers also handle direct services approximately 30% of the time; the rest of their time is spent handling group sessions and overseeing the direct services offered by the social workers. The house managers supervise the facility and maintain the grounds, take telephone referrals, assist families with check-in, establish housekeeping obligations, and supervise the volunteer program. The executive director oversees all functions of the House, staffs the Board of Directors (including fund raising, speaking engagements, finance, and house operations), prepares budget materials and grant and funding applications, supervises staff, interacts with the community to encourage referrals, and receives community responses to the program. The executive director maintains statistics in client services and advocates as needed throughout the community for the needs associated with the client population.

The Family House's staff feel that the supervision of staff and volunteers is generally good. The House managers feel they have difficulty completing tasks in a timely fashion, partially because of the large fluctuation in the client population and partially because of difficulty in time management. The service delivery is of extremely high quality, and employee retention levels are high.

Resources the staff needs: At this time, staff salaries have begun to lag behind comparable salaries in other organizations. We lack sufficient office space for administrative needs and sufficient private space for client counseling when the House is full. In-service training needs to be increased to keep staff professionally challenged. The managers need training in supervision skills and time management. One additional area that requires attention is the delineation of roles and responsibilities between staff and volunteers.

4.3 Board of Directors

The House's Board of Directors played a strong leadership role in the original program's creation and design. Policy and organizational tasks have been handled exceedingly well because of the roles of key Board members with extensive experience in handling these matters. However, the Board as a whole has expressed a concern about a lack of direction and has frequently become consumed with the details of agency management rather than in seeing the agency from a holistic vantage point. Operational issues have been less consistent and clearly dependent on the committee chair's capabilities and commitment. In the past 2 years, fund raising and special events have been quite successful, primarily because of the committee chairs. However, no plans are in place to train new chairs or Board officers to replace these positions when current terms of office expire.

Resources the Board needs to increase commitment and purpose: The Board needs a workstation at the House with a computer and phone. The Board members need a program for developing leadership skills to ease the transition of committee chairs and officers. The Board needs an orientation packet for new members that clearly explains the time and expertise required to successfully fulfill Board obligations.

4.4   Volunteers

The Family House volunteer program has approximately 100 members. The average length of involvement with the House is 2 years. Most of the volunteers contact the agency to become involved, and very little active recruitment is done. Currently, this does not pose a problem, but as the agency ages and becomes less novel, we may need to institute an active recruitment program.

Volunteers assist with House maintenance, recreational activities for House residents, and travel assistance to work, school, or doctor's appointments. They also provide respite services to children or siblings, thereby allowing parents time to address their own adult needs. The volunteers are quite enthusiastic about their assignments, but they tend to try to offer counseling services rather than their assigned tasks. This is the primary area in which staff and volunteer roles tend to become blurred. Volunteers are good about adhering to their schedules and have recently begun their own fund raising efforts, which have increased their involvement with the House.

Resources needed for the volunteer program include scheduled training sessions on a semiannual basis and some type of recognition device to honor those who devote their time and energy to our program. The addition of the volunteer committee chair to the Executive Committee would provide a greater awareness and appreciation for the program among the Board members. Within the next year, the program size needs to be closely monitored to determine if we need to begin an active recruitment program.

4.5   Facilities and Equipment

Additional office space is needed for administrative staff, clinical services, Board members, and volunteers. The House has sufficient space for families but not enough for the intervention and support services required to keep the program successful.

The House budget needs to reflect a willingness to invest in quality equipment and computer software. Too much time is spent trying to secure donations of used equipment or personally designed software programs. As a result, the equipment and software are difficult to maintain and much time is lost changing systems and equipment while we continually search for something that will actually meet our needs.

The House has recently been redecorated and painted; the facilities will not require major renovations for several years.

4.6 Organizational Structure

Two areas of confusion currently exist within the Family House: delineation of responsibilities between staff and Board members and between staff and volunteers. An organizational chart and updated job descriptions for all parties need to be created. The growth of the program has resulted in changes without a corresponding change in written descriptions of tasks and responsibilities.

4.7 Financial Overview

Essentially, the House has operated well within its budget, and a base of annual donors has been established through a Friends campaign. The House has successfully retired two of its three mortgages and has an outstanding note of approximately $50,000. State funding may be less secure based on recent state financial problems; the $75,000 grant may be reduced in the future. The Board needs to begin planning on a vehicle to replace this base source of income.

4.8 Fund Raising Programs

The Friends campaign, now in its third year, has proven to be a valuable source of ongoing support for the House. The volunteer program has recently decided to begin a fund raising program that will assist the House in preparing for any facility and maintenance needs. By beginning now, the project should be in a secure position in 2 years to adequately meet the House's needs for new equipment and supplies.

The Fund Raising Committee has completed the original campaign that began before the House's opening. A small endowment has been established, but this will require additional work, primarily in planned giving, to allow the endowment to mature and provide substantial security to our House.

The Fund Raising Committee has sponsored several annual special events, including a golf tournament, a family-oriented carnival, and a black-tie dinner. In addition, the committee is pursuing corporate sponsorship for these events to increase the amounts raised.

5 SUMMARY OF MARKET AND OPERATIONAL NEEDS

5.1 Market Needs

The greatest issue raised during this process was the desire on the part of referral agencies and community leaders for a fundamental shift of the existing Family House program. The issue is the length of in-house services versus the length of the aftercare program as it affects the capacity of the House to serve as many families as possible.

Cultural sensitivity and the need for more male staffmembers also have been issues raised through the market assessment. These will be addressed through staff training and an increased effort to hire staffmembers who are reflective of the general community.

5.2 Operational Needs

The House's operational needs were stated throughout the internal assessment and have focused on raising staff salaries, increasing space within the House for administrative and program services, and addressing the fee and reimbursement policies of referral agencies.

6 STRATEGIC OBJECTIVES AND IMPLEMENTATION

6.1 Analyze whether the current length of the in-house program is appropriate and whether it can be shortened, with a greater emphasis placed on supervised aftercare.

A. Create a method to compare the current program to the proposed program by December 199x. *Responsibility:* Clinical Staff.

B. Implement a comparison program to determine whether we can maintain our success rate even with a change in the length of the in-house program by January 199x. *Responsibility:* Executive Director.

C. Prepare a report of findings and results of proposed changes in treatment length for discussion by the Board at its August meeting. *Responsibility:* Executive Director.

D. If appropriate, initiate changes in program and create our annual work plans to reflect these alterations by January 199x. *Responsibility:* Executive Director.

6.2 Increase Board member and volunteer orientation programs from once yearly to twice yearly within the next year. We will formalize the leadership program so that half of the committee chairs and Board officers are new to their positions within the next year.

A. Revise the mission of the Nominating Committee to the Board Development Committee and recruit community representatives to this committee to assist with the development of a formalized leadership and orientation program by June 199x. *Responsibility:* Executive Committee and full Board of Directors.

B. Place the Volunteer Committee Chair on the Executive Committee and the Board Development Committee by January 199x. *Responsibility:* Board President.

C. Designate a Vice-Chair for the Volunteer Committee to assist with the new responsibilities of the Volunteer Committee by January 199x. *Responsibility:* Volunteer Committee Chair and Board President.

6.3 Use existing budget allocations for in-staff training to increase the staff's professional growth. All staff will attend at least one training workshop within the next year.

A. All staff will request at least one suitable training workshop by March 199x. *Responsibility:* Executive Director.

B. Training sessions will be scheduled and substitute staff will be retained to allow staff to attend training sessions by April 199x. *Responsibility:* Executive Director and Clinical Supervisors.

6.4 The agency will evaluate the need for additional space and equipment and establish a priority list and accompanying fund-raising program to be reviewed by the Board of Directors at the annual planning meeting.

A. Evaluate space and equipment needs and establish a price list and priority rating by June 199x. *Responsibility:* Executive Director, Volunteer Chair, and Board President.

B. Create a fund raising program to meet the projected needs for space and equipment by December 199x. *Responsibility:* Fund Raising Committee.

6.5 The Family House will revise all job descriptions and agency organizational charts to include staff, Board members, and volunteer roles. This revision will also address staff salary levels and volunteer recognition program as well as possible implementation of a formalized volunteer recruitment program.

A. A consultant will be retained by February 199x to work with the Board Development Committee, the clinical directors and managers, and the Volunteer Committee. *Responsibility:* Executive Director and Executive Committee.

B. Draft descriptions will be circulated and final revisions presented to the Board for approval and implementation by November 199x. *Responsibility:* Executive Director and Executive Committee.

7 FUTURE NEEDS

The Family House needs to facilitate conversations with the state funding source to determine whether future funding might be reduced based on the state budget.

We need to explore the role of the endowment and how it may affect the organization's ongoing fund raising efforts. The mechanism for handling the endowment, either through the existing Board or through a community fund, needs attention.

8   CONCLUSION

This strategic plan represents the involvement and commitment of the Family House's staff, clients, volunteers, and Board members, as well as referral agencies and community leaders. Our initial success over the past 8 years has given us much to be proud of, yet we envision even more as possible.

The strategic objectives have been chosen with care, a great deal of discussion, and thought. In the rapidly changing environment in which we find ourselves, predicting the results of future efforts is not easy. The many hours of discussion and consideration that went into this plan have provided constructive debate and definitely added a new dimension to our program.

The year ahead will be challenging for all of us who are involved in offering this much-needed service to families caught in abusive situations. The Family House's mission has received new impetus from this planning effort, and we look forward to the upcoming months as we endeavor to enhance our service delivery and provide the intervention so needed by our clients and our community.

Appendix B

Community College Foundation Strategic Plan

1 INTRODUCTION

The agenda for the Community College in the 1990s is bold. The resources, both public and private, required to complete the agenda are substantial. The fruits of the Foundation's efforts to implement this agenda will be harvested for decades, perhaps for generations. This Strategic Plan is intended to assist the Community College Foundation in playing as significant a role as possible in the development and advancement of the Community College. Furthermore, this plan is intended to be the first in a series of continually updated plans that will guide the activities of the Foundation henceforth.

In October 199x, the Community College Foundation authorized the creation of a Strategic Planning Committee for the purposes of:

- assessing the mission of the Foundation;
- gathering the advice and counsel of Board members, the Community College faculty and administrators, and community leaders on the Foundation's proper role and perceived effectiveness;
- reviewing legal, economic, and other trends that may affect the Foundation's future structure and operation;
- recommending to the Board a set of goals with a plan for achieving those goals.

This Strategic Plan reflects the consensus expressed by the Board to move the Foundation forward on several strategic fronts, including (1) leadership in fund raising, (2) a more fully autonomous relationship with the Community College, (3) enhanced Board effectiveness, and (4) strengthening relationships with other Community College support organizations. Furthermore, the Strategic Plan also addresses the need to continue to build on the strengths of the Foundation, which encompass (1) a prestigious and committed Board, (2) the prudent management of the Foundation's assets, and (3) a strong and capable staff.

2 SITUATION ANALYSIS

2.1 Areas of Excellence in the Community College Foundation

The Community College Foundation is fortunate to have several key strengths and assets upon which to build for the future. First among these strengths is the quality, diversity, and potential of the Board members. Furthermore, an eagerness and a sense of anticipation exist for meaningful participation in the life of the Foundation and the Community College.

Second among these strengths is the growing financial asset base of the Community College Foundation. During the 8-year period ending in 199x, the Foundation's assets have grown from slightly more than $1 million to more than $10 million. The resulting impact on the Foundation's ability to act on behalf of the Community College in the past few years has been substantial.

Third, many of the Board members believe that the growing academic quality and credibility of the Community College itself is an important intangible asset for the Community College Foundation. The progress that has been achieved by the Community College among its programs, as well as the numerous awards that the Community College faculty and students have been won in recent years point to the need for a strong Foundation Board to assist the Community College in attracting significant financial support. Furthermore, the Foundation Board firmly believes that the vision and leadership of the Community College President have enhanced the reputation of the Community College. The President's talents in communicating with the Community College's constituencies has begun to result in an enthusiasm for the Community College that benefits from the Foundation's work.

2.2 Areas for Improvement in the Community College Foundation

The areas most commonly identified by the Board members for corrective action include the need for a clear vision or focus for the

Community College Foundation. Indeed, this perceived need led to the creation of the Strategic Planning Committee. Throughout the planning process, the Committee heard repeatedly from the Board and others outside the Board that the vitality of the Community College Foundation in the 1990s was directly related to the task of creating and articulating an exciting vision to which the Board could aspire.

A corollary finding of the Committee was that Board member participation requires attention. This problem has expressed itself in two ways. First, Board members have not clearly understood what precisely constitutes the "job description" of a Community College Foundation Board member. Second, the attendance at Board meetings is low, which the Committee has determined to be most directly caused by the rather routine nature of the meetings. Thus, overall, the general expectations of Board Members concerning both individual and group participation need to be elevated.

The final major point to be made concerns the low visibility the Foundation has among Community College leaders, community leaders, and the College's general constituencies. The low profile under which the Foundation has functioned is not viewed as acceptable by the present Board.

3 KEY PLANNING CONSIDERATIONS

3.1 Economic Conditions

The year 199x, the most recent period for which philanthropic data are available, was challenging economically, perhaps indicating a trend of several challenging years to come. Unemployment rose nationally. In the private sector, real weekly earnings (adjusted for inflation) dropped. Corporate profits dropped 1% before taxes, and business failures rose. Even so, the difficult times have not been enough to stop a continuous rise in philanthropic giving both nationally and locally. During 199x, Americans contributed 5.8% more to charities than the year before. At the Community College, contributions have remained steady.

The surrounding community has long been perceived as lacking in its support for philanthropy. The consensus belief among nonprofit organizations in the community is that, although substantial wealth can be found in the metropolitan area, residents share no commitment to act through philanthropy to meet the community's needs.

In recent years, the Community College has received much of its philanthropic support from corporate and foundation sources. The participation of alumni and other individual contributors has been below the average of comparable institutions.

3.2   Changes at the Community College

The most important change at the Community College that directly affects the Community College Foundation has been the appointment of the new President.

The change in leadership signalled the end of an era that focused largely on building the capacity of the Community College. This physical expansion was symbolized by the rapid development of the main campus. Student enrollments peaked at more than XX,000 students, while continuing shortfalls in the state's revenue projections led to a series of budget cuts that were harmful to the preservation of quality programs and educational services.

The new President has sought to focus the attention of the Community College on continuing to build quality. This agenda has taken shape in efforts to attract the best faculty and students to the Community College, to deepen programmatic and curricular content, to move toward a cultural balance that reflects the community and state, and to become a factor in the community's economic development.

3.3   Regulatory and Legal Considerations

During 199x, lawmakers in several states passed new or amended laws regulating the activities of organizations seeking philanthropic support. In large part, these initiatives dealt with the use of paid or contracted solicitors and have had minimal impact on community college-related foundations.

Recent years, however, have seen direct challenges to private foundations affiliated with public institutions. These challenges have come from media as well as state governments seeking access to private foundation records. Many such foundations have taken steps to ensure more functional independence, thereby protecting themselves from such legal challenges.

Federally, the trend in the past few years has been to amend the tax laws in ways that make it less attractive for individuals to make philanthropic contributions. The net effect of these changes, however, has not slowed overall individual giving.

4   SETTING A DIRECTION FOR THE FUTURE

4.1   Mission Statement

The mission of the Community College Foundation is to assist and promote the development of the Community College by serving as the principal agent through which all major gifts are solicited, managed, and disbursed.

4.2   The Community College Foundation in the 1990s

As a prelude to setting goals for the 1990s for the Community College Foundation, we must set forth a vision of how we wish to assess the organization at the end of this decade. That vision is stated as follows:

- The Community College Foundation is a fully independent nonprofit organization that acts as the principal agent through which contributions are made to benefit the Community College.
- The Foundation is professionally staffed.
- The Foundation Board is well versed regarding the Community College's programs, accomplishments, goals, and need for private assistance.
- The Board acts to marshal the energies of its volunteers and other support groups to attract private support for the Community College. The result of these efforts is a consistent and rapid growth of contributions and of the corpus of the endowments managed by the Foundation.
- The Foundation functions in cooperation with the Community College.
- The Foundation is responsive and communicative with the community as it engages more and more people to participate in the support of the Community College.
- The Foundation embraces the highest possible ethical standards in the conduct of its affairs.

5   THE COMMUNITY COLLEGE FOUNDATION GOALS

5.1   Fund Raising

The Foundation has the following fund raising goals:

1. Increase Foundation endowment funds to a minimum of $XX million by the year 2000.
2. Plan and implement a major fund raising campaign for the Community College.
3. Increase total giving to the Foundation.

5.2   Asset Management

The Foundation has the following asset-management goals:

1. Maintain the purchasing power of endowment income and protect the real value of the endowment corpus.

2. Maximize short-term and intermediate term rates of return in accordance with investment policies approved by the Board.

5.3   Board Development and Effectiveness

The Foundation has the following goals relative to the Board:

1. Increase the Board's knowledge and familiarity with the Community College and its programs and leadership.
2. Increase each Board member's knowledge and understanding of the Foundation's objectives and operations.
3. Increase Board members' participation in Foundation activities and operations.

5.4   Foundation Autonomy

The Foundation has the following goal relative to autonomy:

1. Create and maintain an appropriate, long-term, and cooperative relationship with the Community College.

5.5   Relationships with Other Support Organizations

The Foundation has the following goal relative to other community organizations:

1. Assume a leadership role in coordinating the activities of all fund raising groups affiliated with the Community College.

5.6   Visibility

The Foundation has the following goals relative to its visibility:

1. Promote a close working relationship with the Community College's administrators and faculty.
2. Assume a leadership role in communicating the Community College's mission, programs, activities, and accomplishments to the community.

6   STRATEGIES

6.1   Committee Structure

The Community College Foundation will implement a committee structure that will address the major strategic issues identified by the Strategic Planning Committee. Initially, this structure will consist of the following committees: Executive Committee, Campaign Planning Committee, Finance Committee, Board Leadership and Membership Committee, Real Estate Committee, Program Committee, and Ad Hoc Committee on Autonomy.

6.2   Operational Strategies

The Community College Foundation Board shall implement new operational strategies to assist itself in meeting its goals. These operational improvements shall include:

1. Conducting Foundation Board meetings on the Community College's campus.
2. Revising the format of the Foundation Board meetings to emphasize greater content regarding the Community College and opportunities for in-depth discussions.
3. Implementing procedures whereby the delivery of materials necessary for meetings of the Board and its committees is ensured well before the conduct of business.
4. Encouraging member attendance at Board meetings.

6.3   Committee Strategies

Campaign Planning Committee.   The purpose of the Campaign Planning Committee is to work with the Community College in developing a fund raising campaign plan. Among the issues that the plan must address are the Community College's priorities, fund raising goals, identification of lead gifts and major gift prospects, establishment of a campaign budget and calendar, and creation of a volunteer leadership structure to implement the campaign. The strategies of this committee are as follows:

1. Engage the Community College and the community in a comprehensive planning process to identify the needs, priorities, goals, budget, and calendar for conducting a major fund raising campaign on behalf of the Community College.
2. Assess the capabilities of the Foundation, other Community College support groups, and the Community College to implement the plan and recommend the necessary improvements or modifications.
3. Seek and identify major gift prospects for the campaign.
4. Develop and implement a program to train key volunteers in fund raising.
5. Identify and recruit volunteer leadership to implement the campaign under the auspices of the Foundation.

Finance Committee.   The purpose of the Finance Committee is to establish investment policy and monitor financial reporting. The committee monitors the compliance and performance of the Foundation's investment managers. The Finance Committee shall implement the following strategies:

1. Investigate, review, recommend, and implement the most advantageous and prudent policies for the investment, handling, and disbursement of Foundation assets.
2. Require and review audits of all Foundation accounts and financial procedures and transactions.

Board Leadership and Membership Committee. The purpose of the Board Leadership and Membership Committee is to identify and recruit new Board members, nominate new Board members and officers, establish a Board member job description, create a long-range plan for Board development, implement a comprehensive Board orientation and continuing-education program, and implement other activities helpful to the Board's effective functioning. The Board Leadership and Membership Committee shall implement the following strategies:

1. Revise the Community College Foundation Board Handbook as needed.
2. Create a Board directory.
3. Plan and implement a Board orientation program.
4. Plan and implement a continuing-education program for the Board.
5. Develop a plan for Board recruitment and future Board leadership.
6. Develop a job description for Board members.
7. Review Board policies regarding terms and qualifications for emeritus status and recommend changes if appropriate.

Real Estate Committee. The purpose of the Real Estate Committee is to actively pursue real estate opportunities and acquisitions and develop creative ways of managing real estate gifts and investments. The Real Estate Committee shall implement the following strategies:

1. Develop and implement a plan for real estate acquisition, management, and development.
2. Aggressively seek gifts of real estate.

Program Committee. The purpose of the Program Committee is to develop and implement mutually beneficial relationships and activities among the Foundation, the Community College, and the community. The Program Committee shall implement the following strategies:

1. Develop and implement a comprehensive plan for promoting the Foundation and the Community College in the community.

2. Develop and implement a program of interaction between the Foundation Board and key Community College administrators, faculty, and students.

Ad Hoc Committee on Autonomy.   The purpose of the Ad Hoc Committee on Autonomy is to advise the Board concerning the most appropriate relationship between the Foundation and the Community College. The Ad Hoc committee shall implement the following strategy:

1. Plan and recommend the procedures, resources, and relationships needed to ensure the best possible relationship with the Community College.

7   MONITORING AND ACCOUNTABILITY

It shall be the responsibility of the committees to report to the full Board regarding their progress in implementing these strategies semiannually or more frequently as required. Furthermore, the Board may elect at anytime to revise this plan.

8   CONCLUSION

The Strategic Planning Committee wishes to express its appreciation to the members of the Board, the Community College's faculty and administrators, and representatives of the community who so generously participated in the formulation of this plan.

Index

About the Authors

Patrick J. Burkhart (M.B.A., University of Toledo) is President of Resource Planning Consultants, Inc., of Scottsdale, Arizona, a consulting firm to nonprofit organizations and governmental units in Arizona. He also serves as Vice President of the Arizona State University Foundation. He has more than 16 years' experience in nonprofit management, strategic planning, fund raising, and grant writing with a variety of community organizations devoted to economic development, land use planning, community bond issues, and transportation.

Suzanne Reuss (M.S.W., University of California at Berkeley) is Vice President of Resource Planning Consultants, Inc. She has 14 years of management experience with nonprofit organizations in both the San Francisco Bay Area and Phoenix metropolitan area. She also has produced conferences, assisted in the production of educational videotapes, developed and conducted volunteer-training programs, written grants and taught grant writing, and served as a field instructor for Arizona State University's School of Social Work.